VISIONS OF THE HARVEST

A VISION OF THE HARVEST
by Rick Joyner

WAR AND GLORY
by Rick Joyner

THE TITANIC AND THE STOCK MARKET
by Rick Joyner

ESCAPE FROM CHRISTENDOM
by Robert E. Burnell

MorningStar
PUBLICATIONS
16000 Lancaster Highway • Charlotte, NC 28277-2061

Table of Contents

THE TITANIC
AND THE
STOCK MARKET 57

ESCAPE FROM
CHRISTENDOM 79

INTRODUCTION

"A Vision Of The Harvest" is a brief summary of an extensive vision which I received in September 1987. In this vision I saw a sweeping panorama of events, including an outpouring of the Holy Spirit destined to eclipse every previous move in history, along with many world events due to unfold as this age closes. This summary is an attempt to share the highlights of this vision in an effort to awaken those who will hear to the great preparation required if we are to be a part of this move, and ready for that which is coming upon the world. I have updated this summary to include a few other relative visions and insights that I have received since the first vision. These were included because they complement and enhance the first vision, which is published by MorningStar Publications, Inc. in its entirety, under the title *__The Harvest__*.

To properly understand this vision it must be kept in mind that the events included in it unfold over a period of time, possibly many years. The length of time which passed during this vision could have been five years or fifty; I was given no sense or understanding of the timing. It is obvious that many are already beginning to take place. I do know that whether we have five years or fifty, we do not have any time to waste.

This vision ended with such an abruptness that I knew the end of the vision was *not* the end of the age, and I had no concept of how much time was left after the vision ended.

Since this summary was first circulated I have met a number of people who had received and recorded many of the different aspects of this same vision, in some cases with more clarity and detail. As we have been promised,

"Surely the Lord God does NOTHING unless He reveals His secret counsel to His servants the prophets" *[Plural], AMOS 3:7 NAS.* Rarely has He used just one vessel to reveal His purposes. To have the complete picture we must receive the revelation of any one person as just being one piece of the puzzle which must properly fit with the pieces He has given to others, and of course, must be measured by the witness of Scripture.

"The Titanic And The Stock Market" was a part of that same revelation which was written in the form of an exhortation. This addresses practical aspects of our preparation for the end of the age.

"War And Glory" was a second major panoramic vision that I received over several days in August 1993. This vision illustrates major strongholds that are now operating within the church to create division and destruction. It also addresses certain foundational issues that the Lord is about to confront within the church in preparation for her final hour of triumph and glory.

"Escape From Christendom" is a prophetic allegory first published by Bethany House Publishers in 1980. Its prophetic significance has been resoundingly proven as it specifically foretold the major spiritual catastrophes which befell the church during the decade which followed. However, its lessons are no less relevant to the present and future. Not only did this vision warn of the entrapments of a wrongly Americanized and secularized version of the faith, but it is also a bright light shining on the path to the true city of God. We believe that this is destined to become a great classic of Christian literature.

Together these visions and exhortations succinctly identify many of the present and impending major issues of our time. With the exception of "War And Glory," these were formally published under the title *The Harvest Trilogy.*

Believing that "War And Glory" definitely further illuminated the message of the first three, we decided to expand the version with this edition. I trust that together they will be both a challenge and a timely inspiration as we continue to prepare to face the ultimate issues at the end of this age, and to witness the triumph that was gained for all by our Great King.

A VISION OF
THE HARVEST

by Rick Joyner

W hen this vision was first printed in 1987 it seemed that just a few prophetic people were perceiving that the world was on the verge of a great spiritual harvest. Now it seems that the entire body of Christ is in expectation of an unprecedented outpouring the Holy Spirit. Much of the world is already experiencing a harvest. The church in many nations is experiencing everything from genuine revival to what could be termed another Great Awakening. We are truly in the initial stages of a harvest that will ultimately be greater than all its predecessors.

However, even with the almost universal expectation of the coming harvest, far too little has actually been done by the church to prepare for it. When the Soviet Union opened to religious freedom the sects and cults were very well prepared to sweep in with strategy and discipline. It has taken the church almost five years to respond to this great opportunity with even comparable resources. We are now on the verge of seeing the two greatest harvest fields in the world open, China and the Middle East. Again, the church seems halting and timid in preparing for these great opportunities, while the sects and cults are mobilized with great resolve to fill the void.

Not only are these previously closed fields about to open, but Europe and the United States are also on the verge of another Great Awakening. Vast multitudes of nominal believers are about to come into the fold, followed by multiplied millions of new believers who will be smitten by the reality of the Lordship of Jesus Christ.

With this conviction, I have rewritten this summary of the vision adding practical applications to what I was shown. Visions and prophetic revelations that are trumpeted accomplish little if they do not make a "distinct sound" so that we know why we are to rally. True revival and the ingathering of new souls into the kingdom are tremendous blessings, but if we are unprepared, they can result in great tragedies.

The church in some parts of the world is already growing at an incomprehensible rate. The Holy Spirit has been witnessing about the coming harvest on an almost universal basis because it will ultimately be universal. The more prepared that we are for it, the more effective we will be in gathering this great harvest for the Lord. The more unprepared that we are for the time of harvest, the more fruit that will be lost or will go ungathered. Here we are not just talking about apples or wheat in a field, we are talking about human beings.

The Coming Tidal Wave

On May 11, 1992 I saw the church like a surfer floating on a short surfboard, gazing at the beach, lazily drifting and dreaming of the big wave. While this surfer was drifting, the very wave of which he was dreaming was getting closer and closer but he did not know it. I knew that unless he woke up and looked around very fast it was going to come crashing down on top of him and the result was not going to be a smooth ride! I also knew that his board was too short for the huge wave that was coming. It was clear that because of his lethargy, the very wave this surfer dreamed of placed him in serious jeopardy. By the time he did hear the sound of the wave and turned to look, it was too late. What had been the desire of his heart became a terror because, when it came, he was not ready for it. The wave turned the surfer over and over, smashing him into the bottom several times and breaking his board. I feared for his life but he did survive, with many cuts, bruises, and a few broken bones.

I watched the surfer lying on the beach in great pain. Soon the terror of looming death passed and a deep wisdom replaced it. He gazed back out over the sea. Even though he was so broken and hurt that he could hardly move, an awesome resolve and dignity came over him. I knew he would come back to ride the waves again.

I then saw this surfer in a hospital room looking over the ocean. He was still gazing out over the sea, but I knew that instead of dreaming, he was now planning. I then saw him standing on the beach, not only healed but far more muscular than he had been before. Next to him stood the largest surfboard I have ever seen. Even though the sea was calm, I knew and he knew that the biggest wave of all was already in motion beyond the horizon. He was ready in that he could ride the wave, but fears were rising up in him. I knew that if he did not quickly dismiss them and get moving, he would not be able to paddle out far enough in time and would again be in great jeopardy from the wave.

There were also many other surfers who looked like professional body builders standing all over the beach. These all had the same kind of short boards that the original surfer had at first. These body builders seemed uninterested in the waves, but were busy showing off their bodies, which really looked grotesque. I knew that their large, bulging muscles had been artificially contrived, and were, in truth, not as strong as the real surfer's, whose muscles seemed more natural.

Interpretation

In the previous great awakenings or revivals in church history there have been very few individuals who were anticipating the move of the Holy Spirit. In most every great awakening or revival, the existing churches and ministries were damaged by the new move simply because they were not ready for it. Some of these had to actually resist the revival just to survive. In contrast, today there seems to be almost a universal expectation of impending revival, but there has been very little actual preparation for it. Even though we may know it is coming, it seems we have been spending more time dreaming about it than preparing for it. The wave of the Holy Spirit that is coming is in reality bigger than we have imagined, but because we are dreaming instead of looking and preparing, we are now in serious jeopardy from the very wave we have been hoping to see.

That the first surfboard was so short, and clearly inadequate for even a good size wave, much less the awesome one that came, speaks of the inadequacy of the current vehicles, outreaches and ministries of the church. I felt that even if the surfer had seen the wave in time, he could not have maneuvered it. He would have been forced to quickly paddle either toward the beach, or out beyond its breaking point. He would have been forced, from one position or the other, to watch it go by.

Like this surfer, the present church is in danger of getting nothing more than a good beating and a good lesson out of the impending move of the Holy Spirit. Even though the church has been hearing from the Lord about the coming ingathering, we have not been acting on His words nor taking practical steps to be ready for what is ahead. But this beating will immediately bring a wisdom and resolve to become ready for the next wave, and to have the proper vehicle for riding it. The time we spend recovering from the injuries of the wave that is upon us must be spent in planning for the next one; then, our plans must be turned into action.

To ride the wave that is coming we will also need to be, as a corporate body, much stronger than we are now. Strength comes from *exercising* and *proper nutrition*. When the surfer returned to the beach he had the physique of a body builder, but one who had built himself up for strength and not just show. Every muscle was perfectly formed and powerful.

The body of Christ must likewise be built up. Every muscle and every limb, or every individual part of the body, must be properly exercised and brought to full strength. For decades we have been preaching on Ephesians, chapter four, concerning the equipping of the saints for the work of service, but it is now time to start doing it. This must not be done for show either, to just exhibit our beautiful body. We must endeavor with focused attention to make ourselves ready for the next move of the Holy Spirit.

The Ephesians four emphasis of equipping the saints will again become fashionable. Many will become involved in this "spiritual body building" just for show. These will in truth be devoted more to impressing each other than to preparing for the next move of the Spirit. They will not really have the proper equipment for, or even be aware of, what is going on in the sea (mass humanity). Those who build their congregations for show will actually look grotesque and will not have the proper skills for handling the wave of the Spirit; they may not even be in the water when it comes.

Even though this surfer was sufficiently prepared and had a proper board for riding the next wave, the enemy used the negative experience of the previous wave to assault him with a fear that could have hindered him from accomplishing all that he had prepared for. All of our preparation and work will come to nothing if we are not utterly committed to getting back in the water and walking by faith, not by fear. To catch the wave we must:

—Be adequately trained and in shape.

—Have the proper board (vehicle or ministry).

—Be properly positioned (having discerned where the wave is going to break and getting there).

—Be watching so that we can, at the proper time, start paddling with the wave.

—Be ready to act without hesitation when the wave breaks.

The church has been in the initial stages of a great worldwide revival that will ultimately result in *the harvest* that is the end of the age. As we see in Matthew 13:30, the harvest begins with the tares. Many of the exposés of evil-doing and sin within the church have actually been a work of the Holy Spirit to prepare the church for the ingathering, which is soon to begin.

Every time the Lord has shown me the coming harvest, He has shown it to me in two great waves. There may be more than two waves coming, but I know there will be at least two. The first one will be so great that almost everyone will believe that it is in fact the great harvest that is the end of the age. But there is another wave coming after it that will be much greater. The millions of new believers that will come on the next wave are all called to be laborers in the second one. These people must be properly equipped and prepared for the greater wave.

The first wave of revival that is coming in the church will be a blessing only to the churches that have been using their time wisely and have been truly equipping the saints to do the work of the service. This wave will actually be judgment to ministries that have not been properly equipping their people, or who have spent more time dreaming than preparing.

The Only Constant Will Be Change

This present outpouring of the Holy Spirit will ultimately result in many radical changes for both the church and the world. These must be understood by those who would be used by God for one of the greatest events in history. To those who are diligent seekers of God and obedient to His will, these unfolding events will not be either disruptive or destructive—but will represent the greatest opportunities since the creation to witness the great power and glory of our God. To the obedient, this wave of revival will be but a natural flow of the Spirit moving them to increased light and intimacy with Him. Indeed, we call this an "outpouring," not a "downpouring." What is overtaking the world will not come upon the church; it will come *from* the church. We are not called just to submit to the changes, but to make them!

Those who are comfortable and resist change will have an increasingly difficult time as we progress toward the consummation of this age. Regardless of all of the great spiritual activity that is at work around the world, the greatest temptation to come upon those who are in the initial stages of revival will be the pull of spiritual complacency. Fire burns best upon dry wood, and in almost every place, revival will come upon those who are dry to the point of desperation. It is during this intense drought that the temptation to become lukewarm will be the greatest. This is allowed as a point when a separation can be made between the fair weather pretenders and those who are steadfast and faithful enough to lead in what is coming. It is easy to be faithful when the Lord is moving in a great way, but it is between His movements when the true leaders are found and prepared. The greatest need for all at this time is the need for diligence and a radical pursuit of God.

The Real Treasure

Knowing the will of God has always been more valuable than all of the treasures of this world. Soon the value of this most basic of Christian benefits will know a period of unprecedented inflation. We will soon see negligent believers willing to sell all that they have to get what we may now take for granted, because it is so easily attained. Psalm 32:6 warns us, **"Therefore, let everyone who is godly pray to Thee in a time when Thou mayest be found; Surely in a flood of great waters they shall not reach Him" (NAS).**

Even if we know all mysteries and every detail of the end time scenario, but are not faithful, obedient sheep who know our Master's voice, we will soon find ourselves in extreme jeopardy. There will be times of peace, and there will be periods of calm in between the storms that are coming upon the world, but the Lord wants us to have peace in the midst of the conflict, and calm hearts in the midst of the storms.

The great salvation that Jesus purchased for us has already provided for a peace that no battle can steal. However, the church in the West is almost completely unprepared for difficulties, and we are still prone to fail even the smallest of trials. Every trial in our life is given to prepare us for ultimate conflict, and ultimate victory. We must now embrace every trial as the opportunity for spiritual growth that it is meant to be. No difficulty comes to any of our lives that cannot help accomplish this purpose.

The Boasts from Hell

Satan now boasts that Calvary may have enabled God to forgive us, but it does not have the power to really change us. Before the end comes, all of creation will know that the Lord has both the power to forgive and to change people so that they again fully conform to His image. There will yet be a bride without spot or wrinkle. It will be an eternal testimony that she was so purified during the times of the world's greatest debauchery and corruption.

Satan now boasts that God claims to be a God of order, but He cannot even unify His own church. The Lord is going to have a church that is "perfected in unity," and will do so during the times of greatest chaos and confusion the world has ever known. This will be such a striking miracle that the whole world will understand that Jesus truly was sent by the Father because no mere man could have done what will be done to restore such a unity upon the earth. As the Tower of Babel stood as a witness to the downfall of man, the church in perfect unity will stand as a witness that our God truly is the God of redemption.

Satan now boasts that men, and even the church, love his ways more than the ways of God. Before the end comes there will be a witness that there is a people who will gladly sacrifice everything that they have in this world, and even their own lives, to know and walk in God's ways.

Satan now boasts that men actually love him more than they do God. The hosts of heaven and hell are about to witness a people who will love the Lord so much that they will no longer live for themselves, but for Him. This will be a people who will count it their greatest privilege to lay aside their own interests so that they can devote themselves fully to working so that the Savior might receive the reward of His sacrifice. This people will be so captured by His glory and greatness that they would find it incomprehensible to even think of their own interests. This great people will soon be known by every angel in heaven, and every demon in hell. The world will marvel that men and women of such a nature lived among them.

The Fishnet

For the coming harvest the Lord is preparing a great spiritual "fishnet" that will be able to hold the catch that is coming. This net is formed by the linking together of His people. The links in this net are the interrelationships of His people. The strength of the net will depend on the strength of their intercommunication and interrelationships. This is not only happening in local churches among members, but between ministries and congregations throughout cities, states, and crossing international barriers around the world.

In Ephesians 4:15-16, we see this principle: **"... we are to grow up in all aspects into Him, who is the head, even Christ, from whom the whole body, being fitted and held together by that which every JOINT supplies..."** A joint is not a part, but it is where two or more parts come together. There is a great fitting together now occurring in the Spirit and it will increase in the near future, on all levels. With every joint there will be great spiritual growth and advancement.

The Spirit is compelling pastors to get together with other pastors, prophets with prophets, apostolic men with others of like vision and resolve. Whole congregations are beginning to visit and interrelate with other congregations apart from their own circles of emphasis. Movements and denominations are starting to interchange with each other as never before. For a period of time this work will be the highest priority of heaven.

True spiritual authority does not start with organization; it starts with family. When the church ceases to be a family she loses her true spiritual authority. The greatest authority for accomplishing true spiritual advances will always come from relationship—with the Lord first, and then with His people. The Lord will always give the greatest authority to His closest friends. All time spent seeking intimacy with the Lord will pay great dividends. Time spent developing spiritual friendships will also pay much higher dividends than time spent developing either theology or strategy. This is not to imply that we should neglect either theology or strategy, but they are not the highest priority or the most effective in developing the true spiritual authority which will advance the kingdom.

Some gatherings of ministries and leaders will seem fruitless to those who are agenda oriented. Some of these meetings will have improper agendas, but time and effort invested in developing relationships and mutual under-standings will bear fruit. Lines of communication are the arteries and veins of the body of Christ. Our spiritual health depends on the condition of these lines of communication, and when they become blocked or if they collapse, the situation can be life threatening.

We must always guard our hearts, but as modern medi-cine has well proven, we can have a very healthy heart but still have heart failure if we do not have healthy arteries which enable the blood to flow freely. Is this not what John meant when he wrote, "**If we walk in the light as He**

Himself is in the light, *we have fellowship with one another, AND the blood of Jesus His Son cleanses us from all sin"* **(I John 1:7)?** His blood flows through the body through fellowship. Because **"...the life of the flesh is in the blood" (Leviticus 17:11),** the more real and vital the fellowship, the more true spiritual life that will flow through us.

As fellowship becomes more genuine in the local church, true spiritual life will flow through that congregation in greater measure. As fellowship becomes more genuine between congregations in a city or locality, true spiritual life and increased authority will be released by them for that city. As true fellowship grows between congregations, movements and denominations within a nation, more spiritual life and authority will be released through the church for that nation. The same is true on an international level— the more unified the international church becomes, the more light that she will have for the world.

Because of bad experiences and improper spiritual diets, many in the body of Christ are victims of "clogged arteries" which threaten their spiritual lives. As in the natural, the remedy to their problem is returning to a proper spiritual diet and spiritual exercise. The proper spiritual diet replaces the "junk food" diet of such things as television, worldly reading material, etc., with the word of God—the Scriptures, spiritual books, tapes, etc. When this is done, the results will be felt almost immediately. When we begin to abide in the light again, fellowship will naturally result, as we read in I John 1:7.

Don't Waste Your Trials

Fellowship always bears fruit. Even when we have difficulties, it brings the darkness of our own hearts to light and allows grace to work in us. This will always result in an increase of the fruit of the Spirit in our lives if we resist the temptation to become bitter or disbelieving. The Lord dwells in a temple made of *multiple* living stones, and as we are more properly fitted together in His church, we will experience more of His presence. This will also begin to draw back into fellowship many who have drifted away because of former negative experiences and wounds.

The end of the age will be marked by governments swinging from the complete control of totalitarianism, to the other extreme of lawlessness and anarchy. The government of the church has been experiencing these extremes as well. Many of the problems and injuries that Christians have suffered have come from church governments drifting into these extremes. The Lord will use this to prepare us for the disintegration of civil government which will mark the end of the age.

We must always keep in mind the fact that God's main business in the earth today is redemption. If He can redeem even the world's most brutal tragedies, how much more can He redeem the well-meaning but sometimes misguided mistakes of church leaders? Some who have made the greatest mistakes will become the most wise and stable leaders as the chaos of the world increases. Simon Peter is one of the great biblical examples of this principle.

The whole of our experience has been meant to make us better, but often we have let it make us bitter. We must overcome the wounds and begin to use the wisdom that we have gained to begin pulling others out of their misery. "**We know that God causes *all things* to work together for good to those who love God, to those who are called according to His purpose" (Romans 8:28).**

One of the requirements for the priests under the Old Covenant was that he could not have boils (see Lev. 21:20).

Boils are small unhealed wounds that have become infected. A person with boils becomes so sensitive that he cannot be touched without pain. This of course was a biblical model of how we, too, can be disqualified from effective ministry by letting our small wounds become infected. Then no one can get close to us. To be effective in ministry we must be touchable.

The wounds of betrayal and misunderstanding accompany life in this fallen world. We will all experience them. One of the primary differences between those who go on to bear spiritual fruit and those who don't, is how well they deal with their wounds. One of our greatest accomplishments will be to learn to overcome them. This is simple, but it is often not easy. The only requirement for healing these wounds is that basic, and yet most powerful Christian grace—forgiveness. If we do not learn to forgive, we are the ones who will suffer.

It is by the Lord's stripes that we are healed. This is not just the physical blows that He received for us, but that He took them without retaliating—He absorbed them. The evil of these unjust wounds was broken because He accepted them without striking back, or becoming bitter about them. His response was, **"Father forgive them; for they do not know what they are doing" (Luke 23:34).**

Whenever we experience injustice without retaliation or bitterness, we, too, are breaking the power of evil in the earth. This is why Paul said, **"Now I rejoice in my sufferings for your sake, and in my flesh I do my share on behalf of His body [which is the church] in filling up that which is lacking in Christ's afflictions" (Colossians 1:24).** This scripture does not imply that Jesus did not succeed in accomplishing our salvation, but that there is purpose in the sufferings that His church experiences while here on earth. Just as we are healed by the authority of His stripes, we too may gain healing authority by stripes that we take. These stripes, or undeserved wounds, may remain sensitive even after they have healed. This sensitivity can cause us to refrain from further contact and nullify our ministry, or it can make us compassionate for others who are afflicted so that we can bring healing to them. When we absorb stripes by abiding in Him, we, also, gain the power and authority to heal by His stripes that we share.

All of the spiritual wounds that we have received were meant to be a basis for increasing our spiritual authority. Much of the first phase of the harvest will be recovering wounded Christians and helping them to turn negative experiences into stepping stones for spiritual authority in the ministry of reconciliation. Those who are healed of their wounds will have authority to heal those afflicted with the same wounds.

Spiritual Wounds and Unity

The world is falling into increasing division and ethnic chaos as their wounds become more infected; meanwhile the wounds of the body of Christ will be healing, transforming their pain into spiritual authority. As the wounds are healed, the resulting confidence of the church will grow, and unity will dramatically increase. This will be in striking contrast to what is taking place in the world. As unity increases, the intensity of God's presence in meetings will further melt all presumption and all of the facades which separate us from union with Him and each other. His presence will stimulate a worship that brings about a Psalm 133 unity—as we anoint the Head with our worship, the oil will flow down to the edge of His robes, covering the entire body.

He is beginning this breakdown of barriers with the leadership because this is where most originate and where they are the strongest. As the walls come down here the entire body will begin to flow together. If the leaders resist this move, the Lord will continue it through the congregations. These will begin to relate to other members of the body of Christ and their bonds will grow stronger regardless of the resistance or warnings of fearful pastors. Some pastors and leaders who continue to resist this tide of unity will be removed from their places. A few will become so hardened that they will become opposers and will resist God to the end. Most will be changed and will repent of their resistance.

Great events in the natural realm often reflect the great impending events in the spiritual realm. Just as the walls of the iron curtain came crashing down in an irresistible tide of freedom, the spiritual walls that have separated believers from one another are likewise destined to all come down. The leaders who do not perceive the times and resist this tide will be overthrown by it and new leaders will take their places.

Stress on the Net

When the walls between people come down and freedom is released there will be the greatest opportunity for both good and evil. As the walls came down in Eastern Europe, some nations resisted the temptation to overreact to the totalitarianism of their recent history, and established governments which were free and democratic, but also strong and stable. Others used their new freedom to vent their bitterness that still festered from historic ethnic wounds, and conflicts and chaos have resulted. Basically, those nations and people who looked to the future have progressed and greatly benefitted from their freedom. Those who maintained their historic resentments turned their freedom into tragedy. The church faces the same potential dangers and opportunities.

Because of these many different pressures, as well as the magnitude of the "catch" from the coming harvest, the great fishnet that the Lord is preparing will be rent many times, and will be in need of almost constant mending. Much of the discord now taking place in the church is being used by the Lord to prepare those whose task in the harvest will be almost exclusively devoted to the mending and binding of this great net. These peacemakers will have a great part in building this net and will have a major impact on the effectiveness of the entire revival. Those that seem to always find themselves in the middle of conflicts should be encouraged with the knowledge that they are being pre-pared for a great work.

Some that were used greatly of God in the past have become too rigid in doctrinal emphasis, or are too entangled in institutional quagmires to participate fruitfully in the harvest. Some of these will try to join the work but their interrelationships will be so superficial that they will quickly be torn from the net with the first catch. Those who are linked together by doctrine or who gather around personalities will quickly fall away. Only those who are joined by and through Jesus alone will stand the pressure this harvest will bring upon the church.

The redemption of so many will bring much joy but they will come with problems which bring enormous stress to congregations and ministers. The cords of unity must be very strong to withstand this pressure. Those who have not learned to take the Lord's yoke, not trying to carry the burdens themselves, will be overwhelmed. Entering the

Sabbath rest of the Lord will become a major emphasis in preparation for the harvest. Heed this word!

True Conversion

A large number who are now considered Christians, even "spirit-filled" Christians, have never been led to the Lord. They were led to the church, to a personality, or to a doctrine or emphasis. Some of these will think they are important links in the net but will actually become part of the harvest, starting over again on the proper Foundation— Jesus. This group includes many well known ministers and pastors. Their humility in this will lead multitudes to question and strengthen their own relationships to the Lord. This will undergird and encourage the entire body of Christ.

Many denominations, extra-local fellowships and circles of emphasis will begin disbanding and severing ties, even those that were ordained by God for a season, in order to take their place in this great net that the Lord is now forming. For some these ties will just be ignored or forgotten until they have passed away almost without notice, because of the greater intensity and substance of this new move. For others it will be a very painful rending as they are persecuted and rejected by those who do not understand. Those who are required to leave relationships behind will soon receive from the Lord many times in return for those which were lost. The substance of the true relationships that will be formed will greatly overshadow the superficial relationships of their past.

Some leaders will actually disband their organizations as they realize they are no longer relevant to what God is doing. Others will just leave them behind to disband of themselves. Ultimately, all circles of ministry or influence with individual identities will dissolve into a single identity of simply being Christians for all who become part of this harvest.

Single presbyteries will form over cities and localities. These will be made up of pastors and leaders from all different backgrounds. Their unity and harmony in purpose, as well as that of the various congregations, will become a marvel to the world. The Lord will give these presbyteries great wisdom and discernment, but there will be no doubt that Jesus alone will be the Head of His church. What is coming will be bigger than that which any man or council of men could control or administrate.

The Lord's purpose in preparing for the harvest is to JOIN, not to separate. The dismantling of some organizations will be a positive and exhilarating experience for those who walk in obedience to the Lord. They will not be just leaving something behind, they will be going on to a much greater work. Those who have fallen to worship the work of God more than the God of the work will have trouble, but most of these will also be set free by the tremendous anointing that is coming.

Those that feel called to attack and tear down the old will not be sent from the Lord. There will be many "stumbling blocks" circulating in the church that will cause confusion and some destruction from time to time. They will perceive themselves as prophets sent to judge and deliver. Those serving in leadership must trust their discernment and REMOVE the stumbling blocks.

To be distinguished from the "stumbling blocks," the Lord will raise up a great company of prophets, teachers, pastors and apostles that will be of the spirit of Phinehas. Just as the son of Eleazar could not tolerate iniquity in the camp of the Lord, this "ministry of Phinehas" will save congregations, and at times, even whole nations, from the plagues that will be sweeping the earth. They will be moved by the jealousy of the Lord for the purity of His people. They will be sent to save and to preserve the work of the Lord, not to tear down as has been the purpose of stumbling blocks.

PART II

For a time, there will be such an inflow of people that even this great net will be unable to hold them all. New believers will then overflow into almost any work or organization that will take them. Because of this, many of these organizations will assert that they are both the cause and primary purpose for the revival. This delusion will not last long because concurrent with the harvest there will be gripping tribulation in the world which will eventually consume them. This is the judgment of the Lord to uproot every work that He did not commission. Virtually every spiritual organization will eventually be destroyed in this great tribulation on the earth. The only spiritual unions that will survive are those that are built on relationship and not organization.

Even though the Cold War seems to have ended, hot wars will increase. Historic ethnic wounds will be the fuel for most of these conflagrations. There will be some nuclear exchanges, but on a limited basis, mostly between third world nations. What appeared to be the greatest opportunity for world peace, the breakup of the Soviet Union, will turn into the greatest threat to world peace. Many Soviet nuclear weapons, and the stockpiled materials to build them, will end up in the hands of terrorist nations who will use them. At the same time a new wave of terrorism, bolstered by high-tech specialists, will reach unprecedented levels of ruthlessness and destruction.

Even with human violence reaching such levels, more will perish by plagues and natural disasters than by wars during the period of this vision. Earthquakes, especially in Japan and the United States, will spark a worldwide economic collapse. Bartering will again become the primary currency for many nations. Large regions of the world will be reduced to a lifestyle more like that of the nineteenth century than the twenty-first.

The very foundations of civilization will shake and erode. Even the world's most stable governments will be melting like wax, losing authority and control over their populations. Eventually it will be hard to find anyone with the courage to assume authority. This will cause sweeping paranoia throughout the entire earth as civil authorities lose their resolve and courage.

Anarchy

Huge mobs will roam through cities, attacking everything in their paths. The infrastructure of the great denominational churches and large visible ministries will be one of their primary targets, and many will vanish almost overnight. Pagan religions, cults and witchcraft will spread like plagues, but these will also become targets of the mobs. By this time governments will have broken down to the point where lynching and mass executions perpetrated by these mobs are ignored by the authorities. Fear and deep darkness will cover the earth, but this will just make the glory which is appearing upon the saints more striking. Huge masses of people will be streaming to the Lord, the inflow so great in places that very young Christians will be pastoring large bodies of believers. Arenas and stadiums will overflow nightly as the believers come together to hear apostles and teachers and to witness the ministry of the Holy Spirit.

At this time few congregations will remain separate entities. Many elders and pastors may be stationary but groups they oversee will be constantly changing. Some of these will be moving on because of persecution and others because the Lord will scatter them to carry His message abroad like seed. Near the end (of the vision) the body of Christ was perceived like a great flowing river sweeping about as freely as the wind. One day there may be meetings in a public auditorium or stadium, the next day in a park, and continually from house to house.

Great meetings that stir entire cities will happen spontaneously. Extraordinary miracles will be common while those considered great today will be performed almost without notice by young believers. Angelic appearances will be common to the saints and a visible glory of the Lord will appear upon some for extended periods of time as power flows through them.

Conferences of apostles, prophets, pastors, elders, etc. will be called and used greatly by the Lord, but without denominating and separating from the rest of the body. Their unity will be in Jesus and He alone will be the Head of His church. Eventually, the Lord's presence will be so great during this revival that, like the twenty-four elders in Revelation, all crowns will be cast at His feet and spiritual presumption will be unthinkable.

Those in leadership will be the most humble of all. Those who presume leadership without calling will be apparent to all. The leaders of this move will be true servants, not interested in reputation or position. Their humility will open them to become channels for wave after wave of living water (see Isaiah 66:1,2).

This harvest will be so great that no one will look back at the early church as a standard; all will be saying that the Lord has saved His best wine for last. The early church was a firstfruits offering, truly this will be a harvest! It was said of the Apostle Paul that he was turning the world upside down; it will be said of the apostles soon to be anointed that they have turned an upside down world right side up. Nations will tremble at the mention of their names.

These men and women of God will take little notice of their own accomplishments because of their burning love for the One working through them and the recognition of His accomplishments. Like Jesus, they will flee to the mountains when men try to make them kings or exalt them in any way. Their exaltation or authority will not come through man, it will only come from above.

As the masses will be seeking anyone to take authority during these times, this comes as a warning! If the people make the king, who rules? The authority that the Lord will establish will be very different than what even His own people now perceive. We must not try to rule, we must SERVE. Through this His authority will flow and will begin to bring order though peace. Christians will be called on to help establish civil order, but one of the greatest traps set for the church will be the temptation to establish prematurely the kingdom of God through political power. This temptation will be great because of the political vacuum that will be found in many places, but the kingdom will not come in this way. If Christian leaders do not remain focused on spiritual leadership, they will lose the authority that they do have.

PART III

The magnitude of these events cannot be expressed here, neither the chaos nor the move of the Holy Spirit. What I was allowed to foresee ended with increasing chaos and increasing revival.

There will be words and exhortations, originating from the very throne of God and carrying great authority, coming to prepare His church for the days to come. Among these exhortations, we will soon hear His prophets and teachers emphasize the following:

1. WE MUST BUILD UPON THE ONLY FOUNDATION THAT CAN BE LAID, JESUS HIMSELF. Works that are built upon truths instead of The Truth will not stand in this day. Many congregations and ministries are devastated today by the slightest shaking. The works that are properly built on Jesus will withstand the greatest trials and attacks without being moved.

There will be a great emphasis on the Lord Jesus Himself in the days to come. The increasing revelation of Him will overshadow the many emphases of the past like the sun does the moon when it rises. The truths that have been such a distraction will begin to seem insignificant as the church begins to see Him "... **in whom are hidden ALL the treasures of wisdom and knowledge" (Colossians 2:3).**

2. WE MUST REMOVE THE BARRIERS AND FACADES THAT SEPARATE US FROM THE LORD AND EACH OTHER. We must become more intimate with Him, and through Him, each other. Spiritual pride and the idolization of men, individual truths, or works, will come under unrelenting discipline from the Lord and will soon be

understood as "strange fire." Those who continue to offer it will perish from the ministry with such demonstration that a pure and holy fear of the Lord will sweep the body of Christ. This will help the church to move into true spiritual worship and a unity that is based on that worship.

3. WE MUST ABIDE IN THE SABBATH REST OF THE LORD. This will become an increasing emphasis in the teaching and a reality as the Lord enters His temple, the church. Our growing intimacy with Him will bring a peace that will actually calm the storm of the rising sea of humanity. The intensity of the times will overwhelm any pseudo peace. We must be yoked together with the "Lord of the Sabbath," and we must get free of every other human and demonic yoke.

4. WE MUST HEED THE SPIRITUAL PREPARATION WHICH MAY BE REFLECTED IN THE NATURAL. For example: Some have begun moving their assets into precious metals or land. This may be helpful, but it is far more important to take the spiritual land and to lay up our treasures in heaven. The Lord is seeking givers who will become channels of His supply. For them there will be no lack. Those that hoard or do not learn to freely give may suffer increasing crisis in their earthly affairs. This is the Lord's discipline to set them free. Some who are faithful and generous givers may also experience increasing crisis in this, but it is for their preparation to be great channels for the provision of many. Remember Joseph!

Some are feeling they should limit their travel to certain areas and are beginning to emphasize cleanliness because of the AIDS epidemic. This may be helpful, but there is only one deliverance from the judgments of God—to be found in Christ. Spiritual purity is far more important than the natural and can alone protect us from AIDS or any other plague.

5. "THE JUST SHALL LIVE BY FAITH," NOT FEAR. Fears will greatly increase in the world. Actions taken by the church because of fear will almost always prove destructive. Some "faith teaching" has muddied the waters to the degree that some do not even want to hear the word "faith." This frequently happens before the Lord begins a great work. A great revelation of true faith is coming; it will be an essential revelation for us to serve in these days.

Some will be called to walk where angels fear to tread. KNOW that He who is in us is MUCH greater than he who is in the world. The vessels He is now preparing will walk in a boldness and confidence that will astonish a world gripped in fear. Our faith will grow as the presence of the Lord increases. True faith is the recognition of the One in whom we believe. When we truly and properly fear the Lord we will not fear anything else.

Soon many will exist in the miraculous on a continual basis. This will become as natural to them as the gathering of manna was to Israel. Some of the Lord's exploits on behalf of His people will be *unprecedented*, exceeding the greatest biblical miracles. These will seem almost normal as they take place because the *presence* of the Lord will cause more wonderment than His works. He will be very close to His people in these days.

6. THE LORD WILL SOON OPEN OUR UNDER-STANDING OF HIS WORD AND HIS PURPOSES TO A DEPTH BEYOND OUR PRESENT COMPREHEN-SION. The "books" are yet to be "opened" as they will be. When they are, our understanding of even basic truths, such as salvation, being born again, etc., will be enormously increased. This will give far more substance and depth of purpose to the entire body of Christ. The functions of the gifts and ministries will come with increasing authority and

power as their confidence increases with knowledge. The spiritual dimension will become more real to the church than the natural realm. When the proper Foundation has been adequately laid in the church (our union and devotion to Jesus Himself) the Spirit of Revelation will be poured out as never before.

The Charismatic and recent similar renewals were important moves of the Holy Spirit, but to many there seemed to be little lasting fruit. Multitudes who met the Lord were lost again to the world, but the Lord did accomplish what He intended through these movements. He is about to recover many of those who made a commitment to Him but have backslidden. Many of those brought into the kingdom remained and matured. He now has what will prove to be a strong foundation to build upon; He is preparing a net strong enough to hold the catch that He has ordained for the end of the age.

Through the tribulations and dry times of the last few years He has carefully been weaving strong cords that He is now beginning to bind together. The authority on the local church level has gone through many extremes to become mature enough to build upon. Congregations within cities will begin to band together across previously forbidden denominational or other barriers. The citywide church movements will go through many of the extremes and mistakes that the local churches have gone through, but not to the same degree because of the experience gained at the local church level.

The church simply cannot accomplish its mandate without unity. As a single congregation comes into unity it will be entrusted with authority on that level. As the church in a city comes into unity it will be given authority on the broader citywide basis, increasing dramatically over its previous level of authority. As the church in a region or nation comes into unity, it will be given the authority to take *spiritual* authority over that region or nation.

True unity simply carries a level of maturity and death to selfish interests that demonstrates our ability to handle the higher levels of spiritual authority without being corrupted. However, unity will never come just by seeking unity. It will be the natural outflow of true maturity and true commitment to the purposes of the Lord above selfish interests.

Do not resist the Lord in His work to bring unity—it is going to come anyway. Seek greater intimacy with the Lord and open yourself to your fellow members in the body of Christ. Reach out to them and remove the barriers and the whole body will be strengthened. There will always be paranoids who decry all unity movements as the scheme of the one world church. There is a false unity movement that will end in deception and destruction, but it can be easily distinguished. The Lord is not building the unity of His church on control or political spirits, but on love. The true church will not come under a single earthly head or organization, but it will become a single, living organism.

Those who have drifted into extremes will be brought back to the course never again to be distracted from the River of Life by the little tributaries that feed it. Those who have resisted new truth will soon be diving into the River, fearless of rocks or depths. The anointing will soon break all of our yokes. The Reformation showed us the *Way*. Later movements have begun leading us to *Truth*. Through the revival that is coming we will come to know Jesus as our *Life*. When the cord has all three strands it will not be easily broken.

This word is given for the preparation of those whom the Lord desires to use. Relationships are about to be built between ministries and congregations that have feared and rejected each other in the past. He will do this in many without changing their doctrines or emphasis; He will merely cause His people to rise above such differences to worship Him together. As He is lifted up we will gradually begin to wonder how it was possible for many things that were so important to us, and often divided us, to have captured so much of our attention. As this final battle begins we are all going to be amazed, and sometimes ashamed, at those we find on our side.

Humble yourself under His mighty hand so that you may take part in a great exaltation. Those who allow themselves to be emptied, who lay aside all personal ambition to become of no reputation, who patiently suffer rejection and misunderstanding, will soon stir the entire world with the King's message.

WAR AND GLORY

by Rick Joyner

In August of 1993 I received a vision in which the church was represented as an island in the middle of a sea. This island contained many different types of buildings, each of which I understood to represent a different denomination or movement. These buildings seemed to clash with each other architecturally as there were extremely old ones next to very modern ones. There was a war going on between many of the buildings, and most of them looked like bombed out shells. People were still living in the buildings, but most were starving and wounded.

The Controlling Spirits

There were two dark spirits over the island directing this war. One was named Jealousy and the other one, Fear. They congratulated each other every time one of the buildings suffered damage, or whenever people were wounded.

I then saw two powerful and frightening spirits rising over the sea. These became terrible storms. One was named Rage and the other, Lawlessness. They were stirring up the sea and causing great waves to crash into the island. Soon these storms became so large that they seemed even more threatening to the island than the war.

I felt that the people in the city had to be warned about these storms, and several watchmen were apparently trying to do this, but no one would listen to them. The people only argued about whether or not the watchmen should be trusted. This was remarkable because anyone, just looking up could clearly see the storms themselves; however, they were so intent on arguing that they would not look.

These wars had left so many people wounded that the hospitals were fast becoming the largest buildings on the island. The hospitals were congregations or movements that had given themselves to healing the wounded. As the hospitals grew they soon became the main targets of the other warring factions, who had no respect for them as a place where even their own wounded were being treated.

As the war continued, even those who were not badly wounded had the appearance of phantoms, or became grotesquely deformed from the starvation and disease. Any building that grew or prospered became a target for that reason alone. Anytime a building received a supply of food, which would attract people, it would become a target. I began to think that not even the tragic factional wars in Lebanon or Bosnia were as ruthless as this one—and this was the church! I could not comprehend how even a war could be so cruel—*and this was the church!*

Even in the midst of this cruel battle men were still trying to add to their buildings, or to construct new ones, but it was futile. Anytime one building would start to rise a little higher than the others, or whenever construction on a new building was started, it would become the main target of all of the other buildings, and it would quickly be reduced to rubble.

I was then shown many powerful leaders who were conducting this war. All of them had the same word written across their forehead: *Treachery*. I was surprised that anyone would follow someone with that written on him, but they did. I was reminded of II Corinthians 11:20, **"For you bear with anyone if he enslaves you, if he devours you,**

if he takes advantage of you, if he exalts himself, if he hits you in the face."

A Remnant

I then saw that there were people who appeared as lights in almost every building. These lights refused to take part in the fighting, but spent their time trying to repair the buildings, or nurse the wounded. Even though it was impossible to keep up with the damage or the wounded, they did not stop trying.

It was also apparent that each of these lights had the power to heal wounds, and that power was increasing as they worked. Those who were healed became lights just as they were. It was obvious that these individuals who were committed to healing the wounded were now able to do more than the hospitals because of the ruthless attacks on the hospitals. Understanding this, the hospitals dispersed their people as "healing teams" which spread out across the island and moved into many of the other buildings.

There were also many small camps around the perimeter of the island. Some of these were involved in the war between the buildings, and they seemed intent on trying to destroy all of the buildings so that they could bring the people to their camps. The leaders of these camps had the same word, *Treachery*, written on their foreheads. Although they had left the buildings, the spirit of the war was still over most of these small camp leaders as well.

There were a few of these camps which were not involved in the war, and they, too, appeared as lights. These were also growing in authority, but it was a different authority than that of the lights which possessed healing powers. These had authority over events. They were praying to stop small battles, and to keep small storms away, and this was happening as they prayed.

The two spirits over the city and the two storms became very intimidated by these small, praying camps. I felt that these intercessory groups were actually close to having the authority to stop even the major battles and huge storms. This was clearly the source of agitation for these large spirits.

The Tragedy

There were multitudes of boats and ships all around the island that were waiting to enter the city as soon as the fighting stopped. Many of these boats were full of refugees from other wars, and many were wounded. There were also ships bearing kings, presidents and those who appeared wealthy and prosperous. These were all afraid of the storms, but they could not enter the city because of the fighting. Their groans and screams were so loud that I was surprised that no one in the city could hear them. No one even seemed aware of their presence.

In His Wisdom

Then I saw the Lord standing and watching. He was so glorious that I wondered why I had not seen Him before, or why everyone in the city did not stop to worship Him. To my amazement, no one was able to see Him. I then looked into the eyes of some of the people, and they were all so "bloodshot" that I was surprised that they could see anything at all. The blood in their eyes was not the blood of the Lamb but the blood of Cain.

I then wondered why the Lord did not stop the fighting, but seemed content just to watch. As if He had understood my thoughts, He turned and said to me, *"This is My church. These were the houses that men tried to build for Me. I knocked on the door of each one, but they would not open to Me. I would have brought peace because I will only dwell in the city of peace."*

Then He turned and indicated the people in the ships, saying: *"If I allowed all of these people to come to the city now they would just be used in the war. When their cries become louder than the war, I will build a place for them."*

He looked at me with great earnestness and said, *"I allowed this to happen so that it would never happen again!"* It is hard to convey the power of this statement, but it imparted to me a deep understanding that He allowed this conflict to continue from a heart of profound wisdom. He then said, *"Until you understand this you cannot understand what I am about to do."*

When the cries of those in the boats became louder than the conflict in the city, the Lord gave a command and the sea was released. Great tidal waves arose and began to sweep across the island until they covered the buildings. The spirits that were storms joined the spirits over the island, and they all grew to almost double their previous size. Then the island completely disappeared under the darkness of the spirits and the raging sea.

The Lord did not move as this was happening. I knew that my only protection was to stand as close to Him as possible. I could not see anything but Him during this great storm. As I looked at His face I could see both hurt and resolve.

The House of the Lord is Built

Slowly, the storms died down and the tides receded. All of the buildings were gone, but the individuals who were the lights in the buildings emerged and remained standing where the buildings had once been. Then the Lord, who had been on the edge of the island, moved to the center and said, *"Now I will build My house."*

All of those who were lights started turning toward the Lord. As they turned they became even brighter, and each group was changed into a living pillar right where they stood. Soon it became obvious that these pillars were the framework of a building which would cover almost the entire island.

The pillars were different colors, shapes, and sizes. It was hard to understand how all of these, being so different, would work as a single framework. However, the Lord seemed very pleased with each one, and they did eventually all fit together.

The People Come

Then the ships and boats all started landing on the island. There were multitudes of people. Each ship or boat was from a different country or a race of people. I began to think that, even as large as the building now was, there were too many people for the building. Then the Lord looked at me and said very sternly, *"We will build as many rooms as we need—no one will be turned away."*

This was said so sternly that I resolved to never again consider turning people away as an option. I also pondered how the greatest problem before was how to get people to come to the buildings. Now the big problem was what to do with all of the people.

The Cemetery

When each ship arrived, the people on it were led straight to the Lord. He looked into the eyes of each one and said, *"If you trust Me you will die for Me."* When each said, "I will die for You," the Lord immediately thrust His sword right through his heart. This caused very real pain in each one. To those who tried to avoid the sword it was obviously even more painful. To those who relaxed it did not seem to hurt as much.

These were then taken to a cemetery with the word "Obscurity" written over the gate. I felt compelled to follow them. Those who had been stabbed were checked to see that they were really dead before they were buried. Some clung to life for a long time, and were laid off to one side. Quickly, those who were buried began to arise as lights just like those who had survived the storm. I noticed that they were not staying in their tombs the same length of time. Some of these arose before those who were clinging to life were even buried.

When I first looked at this cemetery it looked like a dreadful place and I did not think that it belonged at all on this now glorious island. As I left the cemetery I turned to look back at it and it looked beautiful. I could not figure out what was different. Then one of the workers said to me knowingly, "The cemetery has not changed—you have."

I then looked at the building and it was even more glorious than I had remembered. I looked at the island and felt the same way—it had become much more beautiful. I remembered the Scripture, **"Precious in the sight of the Lord is the death of His godly ones" (Psalm 116:15).** The worker, who was still looking at me, then said, "You have not died yet, but were changed just by being close to those who have. When you die you will see even more glory."

This statement was offensive to me because I felt that I had been standing closer to the Lord than anyone, and He seemed to be particularly interested in sharing His thoughts with me. Even so, deep down inside I knew that there was truth to what he had said.

Those who were emerging as lights from the cemetery were each being led to his own place in the building, which would have his name on it. Some joined the walls, others joined the pillars, some became windows or doors. They remained people even after they became a part of the building. As they gradually settled into their own places their lights began to shine brighter than ever, significantly increasing the light of the whole building.

The Test

I returned to the Lord's side. Standing in His presence was so wonderful I could not imagine why anyone would not be willing to die for Him, but many of the people coming from the ships did refuse. These would all back away from Him at the request. Many of these went back to the ships, some of which left and some of which remained in the harbor.

A few of the people who refused to die stayed on the island and were allowed to walk about freely, even to enter the House of the Lord. They seemed to love and bask in the glory of it all. Many of these began to shine with a glory too, but they never had the glory within themselves—they only reflected what was coming from others.

As I was thinking that it was not right for these to be allowed to stay, the Lord said to me, *"My patience will win many of these, but even those that never give me their lives, I love and am pleased to let them enjoy My glory. Never turn away those who love My glory."* These really did enjoy the house, and enjoyed the presence of the Lord that radiated from the house, but they seemed timid, and retreated when the Lord Himself came close to them.

I then watched as those who had refused to die for the Lord begin to act as if His house were their own, and had been built for them. I wanted to be angry at their great presumption, but I could not feel anger even though I wanted to. I then understood that it was because I was standing so close to the Lord that I could not be mad. This forced me to decide either to stay close to Him or to move away so that I could be angry.

I was surprised that this was a difficult decision, that I would even consider wanting to move away from the Lord, but honestly it was. Out of fear at what was rising within me, I stepped closer to the Lord. He immediately reached out and grabbed me as if I was about to fall off of a cliff. As I looked behind me I was astonished to find that I had been on the very edge of a precipice, and had I taken that step away from the Lord to feel the anger, I would have stepped off of it.

He then said to me, *"In this house I can tolerate presumption more than that anger. That anger would start the war again."* I then remembered the word of the man at the cemetery and was overwhelmed with the knowledge that I had not yet made the decision to die for Him either. I too had been presumptuously feeling possessive of both the house *and* the Lord. When I saw this great evil in my own heart I was appalled and immediately begged the Lord to destroy my evil heart with His sword. I knew that if He did not do it I would forever be in jeopardy of falling off the cliff. I soon became desperate to die.

Resurrection Life

I had always felt love and security when close to the Lord, but for a brief moment, as He drew back the sword to pierce my heart, it seemed that every fear within me came screaming to my mind. I then understood why so many had refused to die for Him, and I felt compassion for them. As soon as I felt this compassion all of my fears departed. I would not experience fear again for the duration of the vision. This deliverance from fear was too wonderful to describe. It was almost as if all of the evil from the fall of man had been removed out of my own heart. I had a brief but brilliant understanding that somehow all evil was united with fear.

Then the sword of the Lord pierced my heart. I was surprised to feel so little pain when it seemed to have been so hard on others. He then said, *"Those who request death die easier."* I remembered His statement in Matthew 21:44: **"And he who falls on this stone will be broken to pieces; but on whomever it falls, it will scatter him like dust."** As I began to lose consciousness I was not enveloped by darkness as I expected, but by light. With the departure of my fear and the coming of this light, death was glorious.

I did not remember being carried to the cemetery, but just as if no time at all had passed, I was emerging from it again. Now the glory of everything I saw was unspeakable. I looked at a rock and loved it. I looked at trees, the sky and clouds, and could not believe how wonderful they were. A sparrow seemed more glorious than any bird I had ever seen. I wondered at the great treasures that all of these were to me now, and why I had not appreciated them like this before.

I then looked at the presumptuous people. Not only did I feel no temptation to be angry, I loved them so much I would have let each one pierce my heart again if it would help them. I then began to think of how blessed I was to be able to meet them and to be with them. Now I actually wanted them to stay and could not even comprehend how I was ever tempted to be angry at them—they were much greater treasures than the sparrow!

Then the Lord stood next to me. Though I did not think it was possible, He was much more glorious than before, and I was able to bear it. He said, *"This is why the death of My people is so precious to Me. Those who seek to save their lives always lose them, but those who lose their lives for My sake find true life. Now you know true life because you know love. What you feel now is the righteousness, peace and joy of which my kingdom is composed. Only that which is done in this Spirit will last forever. Those who live by fear cannot experience My kingdom. If you will dwell in My love you will have the authority to deliver men from their fears, and to demonstrate the kingdom of God."*

I then looked at the house and all of those who comprised it. Everything and everyone that I looked at seemed to stir up this great feeling of love that was more wonderful than anything I had ever felt before. I wanted to go talk to each one, but I did not want to leave the Lord's side, Whose presence was even more compelling. Knowing my thoughts, he said, *"You will never leave My side because I have made My abode in you and I will be with you every-where that you go."*

Those who were presumptuous were enjoying all of the blessings, and even viewed themselves as the reason for them, but they really were not even a part of what was being built. Having just been one of them I knew first-hand how shallow their enjoyment was, compared to what it could be, and a great compassion came over me for them. As I continued watching these people they gradually become thinner in substance until they were just like the phantoms I had seen in the city that had been destroyed. Again I thought of the Lord's words, *"Those who seek to save their lives always lose them, but those who lose their lives for My sake find true life."*

No Limits

Then I looked at how the building kept getting higher; the higher it went the more glory it exuded and the further it could be seen. This resulted in even more ships and people coming through the storms, which were still raging but seemed unable to affect the island. As I wondered how high the building could get, the Lord turned to me again, and as if He were answering my thoughts, He said, *"There is no limit to how high we can build this because I am the foundation and love is the cement."*

This caused me to look at the cement, which was transparent but radiated a great power. I wondered how I had not noticed this before as it was now so obvious and captivating. I then began to ponder how blind I seemed to even the greatest wonders of this building until the Lord directed my attention to them. This caused me to turn back to the Lord, and closely observe everything to which He gave His attention.

The Lord then began looking at the people who now comprised the building. As I looked at them again I was immediately struck by the fact that they were *more* than people—I knew that they were the "new creation" that had transcended this creation. They had bridged the gap between the physical and spiritual realms and were clearly a part of both. They were unquestionably supernatural, which did not mean that they were not natural, but were far *more natural* than anything "natural" I had ever seen. They were more real than anything I had ever considered "real." They made everything else seem like a shadow, and this sense increased as they continued to change.

Soon the glory that was coming from them could be both seen and felt. The feeling was not like a touch, but like an emotion. As I walked close enough to this glory, it made me feel so good that I can only describe it as a wonderful intoxication; not one that clouded the mind, but illuminated it. I felt somehow ennobled, not with pride, but with a powerful sense of destiny. I also felt a profound security, as if I were in complete harmony with the ground, the air, and especially the Lord and His house. This feeling was so good that I never wanted to move again.

With the addition of each new boatload of people, the transformation of those already a part of the building continued, and the glory of the whole building increased and expanded. This made everyone in the building greatly rejoice with the coming of each new group of people.

Sharing the Glory

When those who came from the cemetery took their places in the building those who were already a part tried to give the new ones their own glory. As they did this the glory radiating from the Lord would increase, and He would give those who had given their own glory away even more. Those who were the most devoted to this sharing were the ones used to start the next level of the house, which kept going higher and higher.

I thought of how opposite this was from the jealousy which had prevailed before in the city. I then tried to ponder the jealousy to understand it more, but it was almost impossible to do. Because I could no longer feel jealousy I had a difficult time even understanding what it was—it seemed as unreal as if it had only existed in bad dreams. The joy of sharing was so great that *not* sharing seemed incomprehensible. The more the glory was shared, the more each received to share.

Because this joy of sharing was so great, I knew that all of us would spend eternity just seeking others with whom to share the glory. Then, like a flash, I knew that this was why He had created the universe with such diversity, and why He created it to continually expand at a rapid pace. Those who touched His glory were touched by a love that compelled them to share the glory, which caused them to expand. He had given us the ever expanding universe in which to share His ever expanding glory. He had set in motion a glorious chain reaction that would never end! There were no limits on time or space, and we would need every bit of it!

The Storms Return

Then suddenly my attention was turned toward the storms that had continued to grow over the sea. To my shock they had grown larger and faster than the house of the Lord, and were now coming toward the island.

Great waves covered the island and the building disappeared from my view even though I was still very close to it. The fury of this storm was beyond comprehension, but I felt no fear at all. I knew that this was because I had already died to this world and had a life that could never be taken from me. As wonderful as the island had become, I was just as happy to die physically so that I would be free to carry the glory of the Lord that had so captured my attention, to the rest of the universe. It really would have been difficult to choose whether to stay or to go, so I just rested and waited.

Gradually the storms abated and the building then re-emerged. Both the building and the island were much smaller, but were even more glorious. Then I noticed that the storms were just off shore and were returning. This happened several times, and each time the building would emerge it would be smaller, but more glorious. Each time that this happened the storms were also much smaller—they were wearing themselves out on the island. Soon the storms could only generate small waves that held no threat of any real damage. The glory of the house was now beyond any human description.

Then the clouds dissipated altogether into the most beautiful sky I had ever seen. As I gazed into the sky I began to realize that it was filled with the glory emitted from the house. As I looked at the house I was amazed that there was no damage from the storm, though it was much smaller. Even so, the glory now coming from the house was much greater than before, and was reflected by everything. I felt that it was so great that it must already be extending far beyond the earth.

Then the vision changed and I was alone with the Lord. All of the great feelings were gone—even the love. He looked at me earnestly and said, *"The war is almost over. It is time to prepare for the storms. Tell My people that no one with his brother's blood on his hands will be used to build My house."*

I was trying hard to listen to these words in order to heed them, while still thinking about the great love I had felt. He then said, *"This was a dream, but it is real. You have known everything that I have shown you in this dream in your heart. Now believe with your heart and My love will be real to you again. This is your quest—to know My love."*

Comments

The general interpretation of this vision is obvious, but I do think that many of the feelings that I had during this experience are an important part of the message.

In looking at the different buildings which I knew represented denominations or movements, the architectural clash was so striking that it was grotesque. It was as if they were all so intent on being different that the most hideous skyline had been the result. I could not imagine anyone who happened upon such a city having any desire to enter it, even if the conflict had not been taking place.

The church is doing much more damage to herself through infighting than the enemies without are able to do. At that time I was consciously surprised that the Lord did not intervene in this destructive fighting. Those who were fighting against the other denominations, or movements, were all disqualified from being a part of the house which the Lord built.

It was significant that almost all of these buildings contained those who were true lights. Every previous move of God may have calcified into an institution that seems rigid and lifeless, but all of them contain at least some who truly know the Lord and His ways. These may appear as small lights now, but they will be the foundation upon which the Lord will build His house.

Because the sea sometimes represents "mass humanity" in Scripture (see Revelation 17:18), the multitudes are going to rise up in great waves which will destroy much of the present, visible structure of the church. Those who are true lights will not be swept away by the waves. Those who walk in truth have a foundation which cannot be shaken.

The Lord's command to release the sea did not cause the sea to rise up, but just removed that which was restraining it. The sea then came with such fury against the island that it seemed as though it was controlled by a great hatred. I believe this represented a great hatred that will arise against visible, institutional Christianity, and the Lord will allow it to destroy these institutions.

When these great tidal waves subsided, there were no Christian institutions left standing as represented by the buildings that men had constructed. However, all of the real Christians remained. I do not think that it is wrong to keep trying to repair these structures, as the Lord honored and preserved those who did. Even so, this vision affirmed deep within me the need to focus on building people rather than trying to build another institution that will be able to stand in these times; none of them will stand.

Even though these present buildings were destroyed, they each contained those who were destined to become pillars in His house. The house of the Lord was a brand new building, but those who became the main supports in it came from almost every denomination and movement. The Lord is **"the wise Man who brings forth from His treasures things both new and old" (Matthew 13:52).** The Lord does have new wine to serve, but Isaiah 25:6 declares that the Lord will also serve "refined, aged wine." The Lord will not use *either* the old or the new, but *both* the old and new.

There seems to be a perpetual conflict between those who are always seeking the new thing that the Lord is doing, and those who have settled in one place and are just trying to deepen their roots. The body of Christ desperately needs both kinds of people. After America was discovered there was a critical need for adventurous explorers, but if most of the pilgrims had not been settlers the country would still be a wilderness. Even though there may have been enormous conflict between the two types of people, neither would have accomplished anything without the other.

Likewise, the body of Christ constantly needs those who are willing to press beyond the limits of the present status quo—all spiritual advancement over the last five hundred years would have been impossible without them. Even so, if there were not some who were willing to park for awhile around some of the different restored truths, the advancing church would have probably become so unstable that she would have disintegrated into meaningless fragments.

In addition, there seems to be an ongoing conflict between those who are committed to renewal theology, which is the belief that we can renew the institutional church, and restoration theology, which advocates the exclusive need for new wineskins. It is quite obvious that God is committed to both renewal and restoration. However, we must understand that institutions cannot be born again; they cannot be saved and they will not last forever. He may use them for periods of time to protect and edify His people, but the true house of God is not an organization—it is a family made up of people.

The Lord's house was built in the midst of the increasing storms of rage and lawlessness. It radiated as an even greater light because of those storms. I am encouraged that the Lord will build, on this earth, a church that really will reflect His glory, and that this age will not end until He completes this work.

It could not be any other way. When the Lord threatened to destroy Israel, Moses contended that this would only leave the testimony that He could bring people out of Egypt but could not lead them into the Promised Land. The Lord will have a testimony through the church, which will last for all eternity. That testimony will be that He not only can forgive the sins of His church, but that He also has the power and wisdom to deliver her from sin, and make her into a glorious bride without spot or wrinkle.

> **Now when Jesus came into the district of Caesarea Philippi, He began asking His disciples saying "Who do people say that the Son of Man is?"**

> **And they said, "Some say John the baptist; and others, Elijah; but others, Jeremiah, or one of the prophets."**

> **He said to them, *"But who do you say that I am?"***

> **And Simon Peter answered and said, "Thou art the Christ, the Son of the living God."**

> **And Jesus answered and said to him, "Blessed are you, Simon Barjona, *because flesh and blood did not reveal this to you, but My Father who is in heaven.***

> **And I say to you that you are Peter, ["a stone"] and upon this rock [a large rock or bedrock] I will build my church; and the gates of Hades shall not overpower it." (Matthew 16:13-18).**

THE TITANIC AND THE STOCK MARKET

by Rick Joyner

To interpret current events in the light of Divine purpose is a primary function of the prophetic ministry. God's prophets do not just foretell or predict, but much of their ministry is devoted to the explanation of signs or messages. They often see the relationship between events in conjunction with God's works and His message. There are extraordinary events taking place today which do have a message for those who will hear. Two of these recent, significant events are the discovery of the Titanic on the bottom of the North Atlantic, and the Stock Market Crash of October 1987. As unlikely as it may seem, there is an important correlation between these two events.

When built, the Titanic was a symbol of the opulence and invincibility the British Empire felt in those days. She reflected that period's extravagance, and arrogance, as well as the belief that nothing could sink their expanding world economy and dominion. This attitude is in contrast to God's wisdom which warns: **"Pride goes before destruction, and a haughty spirit before stumbling" (Proverbs 16:18).** In this case, few considered His wisdom, and the subsequent catastrophes of both the ship and the empire are now history. As the Titanic departed on her maiden voyage,

Britain could not even conceive that such a fate awaited her—that in just two years the whole world would be in the flames of war, and that their seemingly invincible empire was about to hit an "iceberg" that would ultimately send her to the bottom just like the Titanic.

Some of the British clergy encouraged the arrogance of the empire. They preached a conservative patriotism because they viewed the empire as the protector of the faith, the greatest promulgator of the gospel, and the greatest moral force in the world. Their spiritual heritage was indeed rich; British subjects who refused to compromise their convictions had impacted the world with revival and the church with reformation. It did not appear that any other country was able to carry the mantle of spiritual authority as did Britain.

Pride Versus Vision

Even so, by the turn of the century the Empire had reached her limits and was resting more on what had been accomplished than on what was left to do. Pride had replaced vision. When this happens the end is always near. The Titanic was just one of many messages the Lord gave Britain to call her to repentance, a repentance that would enable her to continue leading the world toward the fulfillment of His purposes. She did not listen and the empire is no more.

Just as the Lord used the British Empire for a specific period, He has blessed and used the United States in a great way. We helped to reestablish Israel as a nation. We were the primary hedge against the communist plague. Many of the seeds sown by the great British, German and other European reformers have been reaped by the American church and the government. By giving purpose and meaning to the value of the individual, America rose to become one of the greatest nations in history. When we had the power to dominate the world and dictate policy as the lone possessor of nuclear weapons, our esteem for liberty and the free determination of nations would not allow it. We were a nation of pioneers, more interested in going somewhere new or making something new.

The apostle exhorted us to give honor to whom honor is due; we should give a great deal to our ancestors who risked their lives, their fortunes and their sacred honor so that we could live in a land of liberty. Now, as painful as it is to see, the handwriting is on our wall. The most destructive mistake that a great nation can make may have happened to us—our vision has been turned into a pride that rests on the accomplishments of the past. We have begun resting more on what has been done than we are pressing on towards what is left to do.

Paul warned the Gentiles, who have been grafted into the vine because of the Jew's hardness of heart, that they could be quickly removed by their own pride. In the same way, pride can remove us from our position in God's purposes because, **"God is opposed to the proud, but gives grace to the humble" (James 4:6)**. The greatest asset that any nation can possess is God's grace. The greatest liability of any nation is an opposition of God. Our commitment to either pride or humility will determine which we will have. God is able to raise up even the most insignificant nation to take our place. He does not need us; we need Him.

The Challenger Message

The sinking of the Titanic was a warning to Britain to repent of her arrogance, a warning that nothing man can build is invincible. Her recent discovery on the bottom of the North Atlantic is a timely reminder of just how foolish pride will prove to be for any nation. The space shuttle catastrophe carried a similar warning to the United States. The glory of this nation of technological wonders was rising to the heavens one minute; the next she was gone, exactly as the biblical admonition:

> **And I will grant wonders in the sky above, And signs on the earth beneath, Blood, and fire, and vapor of smoke (Acts 2:19).**

The nation was shocked and horrified by the blood, the fire, and vapor of smoke which was burned in our hearts that day, but did we get the message? The Lord did not blow up the Challenger, but our pride did. Pride breeds carelessness. Without repentance this nation can evaporate into a few tiny little fragments just as quickly as the Challenger did. Economically we are primed for just such a disaster.

Is there hope for the U.S.? Of course, *if there is repentance*. With every prophetic warning the Lord is appealing for repentance so that He will not have to send judgment. The judgments foretold will only come if we fail to heed the warning to turn from our wicked ways.

Mercy Triumphs Over Judgment

This patience on the Lord's part is wonderfully illustrated in the Book of Jonah. The prophet declared that the city was doomed, but the inhabitants repented of their wickedness and He spared them. There were many prophecies given during the 1970's about the impending judgment coming to the U.S. From coast to coast intercession went up and repentance was preached, and the Lord did give us more time.

It does not take much repentance for the Lord to relent of His intended judgment. When Abraham asked if He would spare Sodom for just ten righteous men, He said that He would. The repentance experienced by the U.S. seemed hardly measurable to many prophets, but it was enough for the Lord to extend His mercy. The Lord would rather show mercy than judgment. However, one of our most tragic responses to His goodness occurs when we become arrogant because of His mercy, and we fall back into our sinful ways.

It is a mistake for prophets to become like Jonah and mourn because the Lord does not bring down His fire. Let us speak His words with boldness while praying for the people to hear and repent. A single soul is worth more than the ridicule we might suffer because of the perception that our prophecies did not come to pass. Of how much more value is an entire nation?

As words of warning are coming again, many are saying, "We've heard that all before and nothing happened." These do not understand why nothing happened. The Scriptures are clear that times of trouble will come upon the world; we should always be ready. Let us pray for repentance, but prepare for the tribulations. If it is time for tribulation we know the kingdom is that much closer, so we have cause for rejoicing either way. However, we should not be like the foolish virgins who decided to sleep because the Lord seemed to delay His coming. If He gives us a decade or a century, let us use the time wisely. At any rate, we have no time to waste.

The Fragile Empires of Men

The world's wealthy and famous streamed onto the Titanic for her maiden voyage. Because they didn't think she could sink, they sailed boldly into dangerous waters with reckless abandon. This "unsinkable" pride of the Empire proved to be incredibly fragile, as was the Empire herself, as is every empire.

In relation to the present world economy it has been repeated often, and believed by most, that what happened in 1929 could never happen again. It is said there are too many safeguards, a stronger Federal Reserve, higher margin requirements for speculators and institutions, FDIC, FSLIC, SIPC, etc... Do not believe it! We are more vulnerable to a worldwide economic catastrophe than at any time in history, and we are merrily sailing along in the most treacherous seas.

The Fed, FDIC and all of the other safeguards are lifeboats that may save a few, but they are entirely inadequate for the voyage we're on. The owners of Titanic felt that having even half the lifeboats a ship her size should have carried was superfluous. Today's leaders are sailing with the same disdain for reason while touting their ingenuity in designing a ship they think cannot sink. In October of 1987 we hit an iceberg and we are about to see just how unsinkable this ship is.

Students of history marvel at the repetitious cycles of human mistakes. Few have been able to break out of these cycles. Most haven't been wise enough to see anything but what they wanted to see in the trends and events taking place around them. This has also been the case with many that were called as prophets to warn the world and the church. As it was with the biblical seers, those calling for repentance will be lonely voices. The majority who claim to be messengers will always be found preaching prosperity and peace; the majority have always been more concerned with their acceptance than with the truth of the message. Those in authority, by the nature of their power, feel compelled to put the best face on problems. Only the most courageous leaders have been able to hear the warnings and take action. Empire after empire, nation after nation, churches, organizations, companies, even families, continue to fail because their leaders refuse to face the problems until they are beyond remedy.

History Repeating Itself

It is remarkable how the reactions of the politicians and experts after the Stock Market crash of October 1987 echoed the voices of October 1929. After the crash in 1929, the first response of the politicians was to point out the "underlying health of the economy." Christmas sales that year were as brisk as ever. The crash was soon almost forgotten, remembered as a curiosity more than anything else. After the crash the market began to rise again and continued for several years, until June of 1932 when the Depression really began.

Even though it was under the surface for awhile, the economy began unraveling in '29; the ship of state was taking on water. Pressure rose for the government to do something. As much as they tried to do what Wall Street demanded, everything they did only exacerbated the problem. As it turned out the underlying health of the economy was far more fragile than anyone had foreseen.

Watching the response to the October 1989 crash was almost like reading a history book. Now several years have passed and we are still merrily sailing along, the economy seeming more robust than ever. We must discern what is really happening. The economy has not sunk yet, and may not for some time, but we are taking on water and we will sink if we do not humble ourselves before the Lord.

When the Titanic hit the iceberg there was a disconcerting jolt. Almost everyone felt it, but after a minute or two the party continued. No one could imagine that in just a few hours most of them would be on the bottom—the ship was so massive and impressive, and all of the experts had said that it was unsinkable. As well as everything seems at present it is almost incomprehensible that catastrophe may be upon us. The Lord Jesus and Paul both warned us it would be just like this when it happens.

> **For as in those days which were before the flood they were eating and drinking, they were marrying and giving in marriage, until the day that Noah entered the ark, and they did not understand until the flood came and took them all away; so shall the coming of the Son of man be (Matthew 24:38-39).**

> **While they are saying, "Peace and safety!" then destruction will come upon them suddenly like birth pangs upon a woman with child; and they shall not escape. But you, brethren, are not in darkness, that the day should overtake you like a thief; for you are all sons of light and sons of day (I Thessalonians 5:3-5).**

The Stock Market is usually a thermometer which continually monitors the temperature of business. It reflects the value the world puts on the economy. Occasionally it has become a thermostat, setting the direction and pace of business. When this happens it is usually catastrophic. Not since October 1929 has this change come with such force as it did in October 1987. It is no longer just measuring the economy; it is now dictating policy. This can happen only when extreme damage control measures are required.

As Roger Smith, the Chairman of General Motors, stated when asked about the 1987 turmoil on Wall Street, "We didn't just have a tummy ache here in our country; we had a genuine, certified heart attack! If you don't recognize it as a heart attack, and if you don't get on that diet and start doing your exercise, you could have another one and it could be terminal."

Our Economic "Engine"

In many ways the economy parallels the operation of an engine, which is why it is often referred to as one. As a jet pilot I learned to pay close attention to my engine instruments and to know what they were indicating. Even if the particular systems were staying within their tolerances, certain trends could foretell serious problems. If there are erratic oscillations, even though they stay within given parameters, your engine may not just quit, it could very well explode!

The economic instruments of the entire world are not only moving between the extremes, but they have long ago, and by a large margin, departed their safe parameters. The indicators are trying to warn us that this engine may not just gradually lose power when it decides to quit, but it may explode with incomprehensible force. The engine that propelled the development of our present culture could also be the bomb which destroys it. The space shuttle tragedy warned of the same.

It is interesting that the hole found in the side of the Titanic appears to have been caused by an explosion from within rather than from an iceberg's gouging it. The ABC special, "Return To The Titanic," related that a coal fire had been burning on the ship since before she left port. A coal stoker who survived testified that they had not hit an iceberg, but that there was an explosion caused by the coal fire, the truth having been covered up for insurance purposes.

There was no three hundred foot gash found on the hull as historians had expected. So much of the bow has settled into the ocean floor that there may be a gash under the sand, but Edward Wilding, a naval architect at Harland & Wolff who designed and built the Titanic, estimated that 16,000 cubic feet of water entered the Titanic in the first 40 minutes after the rupture. A gash that would produce this result would have an area of just twelve square feet! His calculations posed another problem. If there was a continuous gash 249 feet long, it could be only 3/4 of an inch wide to fit his timetables.

If it were, in fact, a fuel fire explosion that caused her destruction it would provide an interesting parallel to the shuttle disaster. Regardless of what actually sank the Titanic, it is certain that we are sailing along now with some major fuel fires in the economy, we are in a field of icebergs which *can* sink this ship, and we have already hit one.

Complacency is the Threat

Whether the initial problem was an iceberg, or a coal fire explosion, the complacency of the leadership on the Titanic was the biggest reason for the disaster. Captain Smith and his crew received numerous warnings about the ice field which lay directly across her path, and they did not even slow down. Even if they were unsinkable, to hit an iceberg head on would almost certainly cause great damage and loss of life.

When the first rescue ship arrived in the morning, they were astonished that the Titanic had not struck an iceberg earlier. They had difficulty getting to the Titanic's position in daylight because of the great number of icebergs. The only possible reason for Smith's proceeding with such disdain for the danger would have been an incredibly false sense of security. What was her leader thinking?

When looking at the course of Western economic policy for the last couple of decades, we must also wonder what our leaders are thinking; how is that we have survived a catastrophe this long? The only answer is that the Lord truly has His angels holding back the four winds of the earth until His bondservants are ready (Revelation 7:1).

It does appear that we have come to the time when the world will go through the greatest troubles ever known—but these are also birth pangs for the coming of a new age, one in which our King will reign. He exhorted us to know the signs of the times and not to be unprepared. This is not just to save ourselves; we are called to take action. There is much for us to do, but we will not be able to save others if we are drowning ourselves.

No Preparation

Because they believed the hype and the vain boasts of the engineers and owners, the Titanic's crew never held a proper lifeboat drill. They did not have a plan for the orderly movement of passengers to the boats, and most of the crew did not even know how to lower them. Everything had to be learned while the ship was sinking under their feet. This obviously contributed to a much greater loss of life than was necessary. Many boats were lowered only partially full, one with only twelve people. Many passengers just did not believe the ship could sink, and refused to leave the comfort and warmth of her cabins; hundreds of those willing to abandon her were held below decks until it was too late.

The entire ship had been caught off guard by the events of that fateful night, and they paid dearly for it. Will we be caught in the same position? The Lord exhorted us to know the signs of the times, and not to sleep on our watch. Prophets throughout the land are now calling for PREPARATION; the Lord is giving us signs in the heavens and on the earth. He is NOW loading His Lifeboat. **"TODAY if you would hear His voice, do not harden you hearts" (Psalm 95:7). "Therefore, let everyone who is godly pray to Thee in a time when Thou mayest be found; surely in a flood of great waters they shall not reach him" (Psalm 32:6).**

In coming years devastating economic problems will be sweeping the world in waves. Great countries and societies will be collapsing. Like the passengers on the Titanic, the water will lap at our ankles, then our knees; then there will be a mad rush to the highest part of the ship. This will be an exercise in vanity, because the whole ship is going to sink. The entire world system is near the end. But we do not have to go down with this ship, because *we do not have to be on it.*

Our Lifeboat is Greater Than the Ship

So what do we do? WE MUST SEEK THE LORD! I do not mean we are to seek Him for instructions as to what we should do; we are to seek Him because *He is* what we should do. He is the Ark of God through Whom we will be delivered from every flood. He Himself bore the curse of our sin, absorbed the judgment that was ours. If we are abiding in Him we do not have to fear the judgment against sin.

This does not mean that we will not be here, or will not have to endure tribulation. It does mean that even if we are called to walk through the fire, it will not burn us; the floods may come, but our house will be built upon a rock that can sustain any storm.

For years doctrines have been preached which have lulled the church into a deep sleep. They did this by assuring us that those in Christ would not have to go through tribulation. This is contrary to the entire testimony of Scripture. He said that in the world we would have tribulation, and that **"through many tribulations we must enter the kingdom of God" (Acts 14:22).**

Consider the options; would it be better to be prepared and not have to go through tribulation, or to be unprepared and have to endure it? The Lord exhorted us to be ready and watching—to be prepared. We cannot continue with delusions similar to those of the Titanic crew who did not think that adversity could come to them—because then it will.

There is no Scripture which says we will be raptured before the tribulation. There obviously is a time when those who are Christ's will be changed, but nowhere does it say when. Many have based their entire hope on the conjecture of a few men and women when the whole Bible is a testimony of God's deliverance and victory *through* tribulation, not from it.

Corrie ten Boom once declared:

> I have been in countries where the saints are already suffering terrible persecution. In China the

Christians were told, "Don't worry, before the tribulation comes, you will be translated—raptured." Then came a terrible persecution. Millions of Christians were tortured to death. Later I heard a Bishop from China say, sadly, "We have failed. We should have made the people strong for persecution rather than telling them Jesus would come first." Turning to me he said, "You will have time. Tell the people to be strong in times of persecution, how to stand when tribulation comes—to stand and not faint."

His Kingdom Cannot Be Shaken

There is a kingdom which cannot be shaken, that cannot sink. It is a kingdom so great, so powerful, that even if all of the greatest problems and tragedies in history were inflicted upon it at once, the attention of a single inhabitant would not be altered or diverted. In the expanse of God's universe, the entire earth compares as less than a single drop would to all the world's oceans. Except for the tiny little speck called earth, the goodness of God dominates the universe. He is in control. And He cares about this little speck. He even cares about you and me. He has called us to live under His dominion—NOW. In His kingdom all things work together for good (Romans 8:28), in all things we OVERWHELMINGLY conquer through Him (Romans 8:37), and He ALWAYS leads us in His triumph in Christ (II Corinthians 2:14).

If we have the true fear of the Lord we need not fear anything else. The Lord clearly told us how we can build our houses on the rock which will endure the storm (Matthew 7:24-27). There are only two requirements if we are going to do this—we must hear His words, and then we must act on them. WE MUST DO BOTH.

Knowing His Voice

Speaking of Himself as the Good Shepherd Jesus said, **"When He puts forth all his own, he goes before them, and the sheep follow him *because they know his voice"*** **(John 10:4).** His sheep know His voice. There are many voices in the world leading down many different paths. We must know our Master's voice so well that, even if they are all are speaking at the same time, we are still able to hear His voice and follow Him only. All of the paths may look good. We cannot follow a path, we must follow Him. If we walk by formulas or "how to's" we will easily be mislead. It is not enough to know someone who knows His voice; we must know Him ourselves.

The only way you can know His voice so as to distinguish it from all of the others is to be intimate with Him. If we try to comprehend and identify the many voices of the enemy we will be confused and frustrated. I was told of a law enforcement officer who spent each day handling true U.S. currency. After a time he knew the feel of each bill so well that he could immediately recognize counterfeit bills when he touched them. That's how well we must know the Lord's voice; we must become so familiar with it that we immediately know the voice of another when we hear it.

Knowing His voice is crucial, but it will be useless if we do not obey Him. Because of the erosion of respect for authority this has become one of the most damaging problems for those who do know Him. Many of us learned as children, and have taught our children, that "no" doesn't really mean "no" until it has been said multiple times, and even then it can be changed to yes with the exertion of enough pressure. Fortunately, as was demonstrated with Peter, the Lord will sometimes repeat Himself to us; but often He chooses not to. Many times, when He has to repeat Himself, it is costly. Many of the presumptuous attitudes with which we may have escaped in the past will devastate us if we continue in them. It is now critical that we become sensitive to His word and quick to obey.

We must hear the voice of the Lord as He has exhorted us through the written word, and as He speaks to us through the Spirit. Our obedience to the Lord has often been hindered by Satan's first, and probably his most effective, tactic—rationalization. "Did God really say that?" It worked on Eve and has worked on most of humankind since.

A good example of how Satan is using this tactic to spread confusion today is in the area of giving. Some say, "Tithing is law and we are under grace." Others react, "I don't tithe because I have already given everything to the Lord,"(which means they don't give anything). The excuses we can concoct to keep from being obedient in this are amazing. This subject has attracted much of Satan's attention, and the Lord gave it so much of His attention in the Word, because it is a path to the Lifeboat provided for us, to help us survive the coming economic troubles. As He said:

> **Give and it will be given to you; good measure, pressed down, shaken together, running over, they will pour into your lap. For by your standard of measure it will be measured to you in return (Luke 6:38).**

> **Honor the Lord from your wealth, and from the first of all your produce; so your barns will be filled with plenty, and your vats will overflow with new wine (Proverbs 3:9-10).**

There is one who scatters, yet increases all the more, and there is one who withholds what is justly due, but it results only in want. The generous man will be prosperous, and he who waters will himself be watered" (Proverbs 11:24-25).

"Will a man rob God? Yet you are robbing Me! But you say, How have we robbed Thee?' In tithes and offerings.

You are cursed with a curse, for you are robbing Me, the whole nation of you! Bring the whole tithe into the storehouse, so that there may be food in My house,

And test Me now in this," says the Lord of hosts, "if I will not open for you the windows of heaven, and pour out for you a blessing until there it overflows" (Malachi 3:8-10).

Because of the begging, pleading and even threatening by some ministries in order to raise funds, as well as the misuse of them by others, it is easy to understand why so many would reduce their giving or stop it altogether. It is understandable, but it is not excusable. When the Father gave His Son for our salvation He established one of the most basic aspects of His nature—giving. If we are to become like Him we, too, must be givers. Learning to be givers is one of the most basic and important aspects of true discipleship.

The Mark of the Beast

The failure of others does not relieve us of our own responsibility to be faithful. This is not for the Lord's sake, but for ours. It is no accident that the mark of the beast is an economic mark, established to control the ability to buy, sell and trade. **"The harvest is the end of the age" (Matthew 13:39).** The harvest will bring the reaping of everything that has been sown, both the good and the evil. Because **"the love of money is the root of all evil" (I Timothy 6:10),** learning to properly relate to money is one of the ultimate issues of the human heart. Therefore, it will be one of the ultimate issues at the end of the age. We must learn to be givers, not deriving our security from our money or possessions. This is a critical test with which we will be confronted in these times.

As an instrument flight instructor I had to teach what was called the "instrument scan." This is the skill of developing a pattern for viewing all of the instruments simultaneously so you do not become preoccupied with one and lose control of the others. When a pilot's scan starts to deteriorate, the altitude control always seems to be the first to go. When this is corrected everything else will usually fall into place again. The same is true in the body of Christ—when there is overall disorientation it often begins with carelessness in giving. With few exceptions, when this is corrected everything else starts falling into place. Giving is a fundamental precept of the Christian life. Christ came to give Himself, and He declared that as He was sent, He is now sending us.

Part II

Three Kinds of Leadership

There were two other ships which played a significant role in the drama of the Titanic disaster: the Californian and the Carpathia. Together, these three ships and their captains remarkably parallel the prevailing attitudes of leadership in both the world and the church.

The Californian obviously had a reserved and cautious captain. When he heard about the ice in his path, he slowed down. When he saw the ice he ordered the ship stopped and waited for daylight. His wireless (radio) operator began warning the other ships in the area of the danger. At 7:30 p.m. her warning was received and logged by the Titanic. This professional, reserved and cautious captain may have saved his own ship by following his nature that night, but later his caution may have cost the lives of those who perished on the Titanic.

The Titanic crew received six warnings about the ice that night, and they disregarded them all. This tells the story of the carelessness which permeated her bridge. It was not just the captain, but almost the entire officer staff, who received and paid little or no attention to the warnings. When this attitude prevails in the leadership doom is imminent.

The usually stormy North Atlantic was amazingly calm that night. One officer remarked that he had never seen the sea so tranquil. First officer Lightoller of the Titanic made this observation at the inquiry when he declared that "everything was against us." Just as the Lord warned,

"While they are saying 'Peace and safety!' destruction will come upon them suddenly" (I Thessalonians 5:3).

This tranquility must have also overcome the crew of the Californian. Her bridge watch saw the Titanic approaching just a few miles away; then they saw her stop dead in the water. At first they probably thought she was taking the same precautions for the ice which they had taken. Then she started firing rockets into the air every few minutes, always a distress signal at sea. They rationalized this, remarking that it must be a signal meant for another company ship which they could not see. The wireless operator was asleep and they did not even wake him to see if he could contact the ship and confirm their theory. Then they watched her disappear, telling each other that she was sailing away when she was actually slipping beneath the sea.

Had the crew of the California responded to the first distress signal they may well have been able to save all of the lives that were lost. The lackadaisical attitude of her crew that night is beyond comprehension, just as is the attitude prevailing in the world, and much of the church today. When the final inquiry comes and the final story is told, will we, also, marvel at how many were in a position to save many lives, but instead slept right through the night just as the captain of the Californian? As our world sinks into the deep are we going to sleep when we could be saving multitudes, or are we going to rise up and take action?

The Prepared

The other ship in the fateful drama of that night was the Carpathia, captained by Arthur H. Rostron. He was known for his ability to make quick decisions while energizing those who served under him. He was a pious man devoted to prayer. At 12:35 a.m. the Carpathia's wireless operator burst into Rostron's quarters to report that the Titanic had struck an iceberg. Rostron reacted in character; he ordered the Carpathia to turn around and proceed, "full speed ahead", later asking the operator if he was sure of the message, a striking contrast to the reaction on the Californian.

Rostron then gave an amazing display of a truly prepared mind; he thought of everything. He ordered the English doctor to the first class dining room, the Italian doctor to second class, the Hungarian to third class, along with every possible piece of equipment or supplies needed for the sick or wounded. He ordered different officers to different gangways, instructing them to get the names of survivors to send by wireless.

They prepared block and lines with chair slings for the wounded. Bowlines were secured along the ship's sides with boat ropes and heaving lines, for anchoring people in chairs. All gangway doors were opened. He then directed specific officers to be in charge of his present passengers, to take care of their needs and to keep them out of the way. All hands were to prepare coffee, soup and provisions. He then designated that all officer's cabins, smoke rooms, library, etc., be used to accommodate the survivors. Stewards were sent to reassure and explain to their own passengers the reason for the activity to help keep them calm.

Heroes Know No Obstacles

Then Rostron turned to face the biggest problem of all, the ice. He was heading at full speed into the same field that had stopped the Titanic. To him reducing speed was out of the question, but he took every measure to reduce the risk to his own ship and passengers. He added a man to the crow's nest, put two more on the bow, one on each wing of the bridge, and he stayed there himself. His second officer, James Bisset, then watched the captain taking one last, but most important, measure—he prayed.

At 2:45 a.m. Bisset saw the first iceberg. They steered around it and kept going. The next hour they dodged five more. At 4:00 a.m. they reached the Titanic's last called position and began picking up lifeboats. As the sun rose it revealed an astonishing sight; the sea was full of icebergs for as far as the eye could see! Even with all the lookouts, the Carpathia had passed numerous bergs which they had not even seen. No one could imagine how they missed them all, except the captain, who knew very well who his Helper was.

The difficult rescue of the survivors was carried out with such order and discipline that peace reigned over all. The Carpathia's passengers caught the spirit of self-sacrifice. The first class passengers gave their own quarters to survivors; others were pitching in to do all they could. On one of the darkest nights of tragedy ever experienced on the high seas, the Carpathia's captain, crew and passengers stand out as bright lights of courage and heroism. They are a demonstration of what the Lord has called us to be in the night of tragedy and loss that is now falling upon the earth. Let us not sleep as some did, or be fooled by the present calmness of the sea. Let us be PREPARED. As the prophet Daniel foresaw, **"The people who know their God will display strength and take action" (Daniel 11:32).**

ESCAPE FROM CHRISTENDOM

by Robert E. Burnell

The Journey

In my dream I see the lone figure of a man following a road. As the sun sets beneath the hills, a city comes into view. Nearing it, the traveler sees what appears to be a large group of churches. Spires and crosses pierce the skyline. His pace quickens. Is this his destination? He passes an imposing structure, a neon sign flashing "Cathedral of the Future." Farther on a floodlit stadium supports a billboard boasting that fifty thousand people crowd into evangelistic meetings there three nights a week. Beyond this, modest "New Testament" chapels and Hebrew Christian synagogues cluster together on the street front.

"Is this the City of God?" I hear the traveler ask a woman at the information booth in the central square.

"No, this is Christian City," she replies.

"But I thought this road led to the City of God!" he exclaims with great disappointment.

"That's what we all thought when we arrived," she answers, her tone sympathetic.

"This road continues up the mountain, doesn't it?" he asks.

"I wouldn't know, really," she answers blankly.

I watch the man turn away from her and trudge on up the mountain in the gathering darkness. Reaching the top, he stares out into the blackness; it looks as though there is nothing, absolutely nothing, beyond. With a shudder he retraces his steps into Christian City and takes a room at a hotel.

Strangely unrefreshed, at dawn he arises and follows the road up the mountain again; in the brightening light of the sun he discovers that what seemed like a void the night before is actually a desert—dry, hot, rolling sand as far as the eye can see. The road narrows to a path which rises over a dune and disappears. "Can this trail lead to the City of God?" he wonders aloud. It appears to be quite deserted and rarely traveled.

Indecision slowing his steps, he again returns to Christian City and has lunch in a Christian restaurant. Over the music of a gospel record, I hear him ask a man at the next table, "That path up the mountain, where the desert begins, does it lead to the City of God?"

"Don't be a fool!" his neighbor replies quickly. "Everyone who has ever taken that path has been lost... swallowed up by the desert! If you want God, there are plenty of good churches in this town. You should pick one and settle down."

After leaving the restaurant, looking weary and confused, the traveler finds a spot under a tree and sits down. An ancient man approaches and begins pleading with him in urgent tones, "If you stay here in Christian City, you'll wither away. You must take the path. I belong to the desert you saw earlier. I was sent here to encourage you to press on. You'll travel many miles. You'll be hot and thirsty; but angels will walk with you, and there will be springs of water along the way. And at your journey's end you will reach the City of God! You have never seen such beauty! And when you arrive the gates will open for you, for you are expected."

"What you say sounds wonderful," the traveler replies. "But I'm afraid I'd never survive that desert. I'm probably better off here in Christian City."

The ancient one smiles. "Christian City is the place for those who want religion but don't want to lose their lives. The desert is the territory of those whose hearts are so thirsty for God that they are willing to be lost in Him. My friend, when Peter brought his boat to land, forsook all and followed Jesus, he was being swallowed by the desert. When Matthew left his tax collecting and Paul his Pharisaism, they too were leaving a city much like this to pursue Jesus out over the dunes and be lost in God. So don't be afraid. Many have gone before you."

Then I see the traveler look away from the old man's burning eyes to the bustle of Christian City. He sees busy people hurrying hither and yon with their Bibles and shiny attaché cases, looking like men and women who know their destiny. But it is clear they lack something which the old man with eyes like a prophet possesses.

In my dream I imagine the traveler turning things over in his mind. "If I do go out there, how can I be sure that I will really be lost in God? In the Middle Ages Christians tried to lose themselves in God by putting the world behind them and entering a monastery. And how disappointed many of them were to find that the world was still there! And the people here in Christian City who are preparing to go to some jungle or a neglected slum, maybe they're coming closer to what it means to be lost in God. But then, a person can travel to the ends of the earth and not lose himself."

The traveler turns again to see the old person starting up the road for the narrow path down to the desert's edge. Suddenly, his decision mobilizes him and he leaps to his feet, chasing after him. When he catches up, they exchange no words. The ancient man makes an abrupt turn to the right and guides him up still another slope which steepens as it rises toward a peak shrouded in a luminous cloud. The climb upward is a very difficult one. The traveler appears dizzy and begins to stagger. His guide pauses and offers him a drink from a flask hanging over his shoulder. Panting, he drinks it in great gulps. "No water ever tasted sweeter than this," he says with great feeling. "Thank you."

"Now look there." The old man points beyond them to a vista not nearly as monotonous and desolate as it had seemed earlier. The desert below has taken on many colors and gradation. In the far distance a blazing light is throbbing and moving on the surface of the horizon like a living thing. "There is the City of God! But before you reach it, you will have to pass through those four wildernesses you see. Directly below us is the Wilderness of Forgiveness." The traveler notices small, dim figures making their way slowly in the direction of the city, separated from each other by many miles.

"How can they survive the loneliness?" asks the traveler. "Wouldn't they benefit from traveling together?"

"Well, they aren't really alone. Each one of them is accompanied by the forgiveness of God. They are being swallowed by the desert of the Lord God's vast mercy. The Holy Spirit is saying to them as they travel, 'Behold, the Lamb of God, who takes away the sin of the world!' They are made whole as they travel."

Just beyond there is an expanse of blue. "Is it sea?" inquires the traveler.

"It looks like water, but it's a sea of sand. That's the Wilderness of Worship. Here, look through these glasses and you will see that people are walking there, too. Notice how they begin to group themselves here. They are having their first taste of the joy of the City—worship. They are discovering how they were made for the worship of God. It is becoming their life, the white-hot source of everything they do."

"But don't people also worship back in Christian City? What's so special about that wilderness?"

"Worship, (that is) true worship, can begin only when a life has been utterly abandoned to the desert of God's presence. Out there the heart begins to worship the Father in spirit and truth."

Looking beyond the blue wilderness to where the desert rises in red and fiery mountains, the old man explains to the traveler that among those reddish mountains is the Wilderness of Prayer.

"Passing through that wilderness travelers find it necessary to turn away from every distraction and concentrate on prayer. They quickly learn that there is no possible way for them to survive but by crying out to God continuously. By the time they reach the outer extremes of that wilderness, prayer is their consuming passion and their supreme joy. It appears at first that the City of God is just beyond the Wilderness of Prayer. But there is one more wilderness hidden by those mountains, which you will pass through before you reach your destination. It is simply called the Harvest. You'll know it when you reach it. And beyond the Harvest is the City itself. Your name is known there. Your arrival is awaited with eagerness. Come, let's begin our journey."

"Nightfall doesn't seem to be a particularly propitious time to begin a journey like this," he says.

"Don't go back to Christian City," the old man exhorts, gazing at him earnestly.

"Not even at this hour? That way I could get a good night's sleep and start first thing in the morning," the traveler adds hopefully.

"But your rest is out there," he urges. "Walk on now, into the desert. The Holy Spirit will help you. Don't be afraid to be lost in God. You'll find your life nowhere else."

The Wilderness of Forgiveness

The old man has left the traveler standing alone at the edge of the desert as darkness falls. The lights of Christian City beckon from behind him. I can imagine him thinking of the warmth of a friendly conversation over a warm meal and of going to sleep in a comfortable bed. But then his expression becomes resolute and he murmurs, "This is doubtless the road I have to take. I will find my life only by losing it, that's a certainty. But how can I KNOW that if I take this path into the desert I will assuredly be lost in God and not merely lost? I can remember many people who took a solitary path which led them not to the City of God but into such unreal thoughts and spurious experiences that their minds and lives were destroyed. Surely the danger of settling for less than life, in Christian City, has to be weighed against the possibility of losing it in a wilderness of spiritual delusion. I'm sure that the darkness beyond contains not only the path to the City of God but also countless trap doors to hell, where one can be lost in lonely vanity. How can I be sure of distinguishing the true path?"

What I first think in my dreams to be a star hanging low over the horizon now takes the shape of a cross hanging directly above the path in front of the traveler. He looks up and notices it, his face showing recognition. He whispers quietly, "Forgiveness." And with deep reverence quotes: "'So Jesus also suffered outside the gate in order to sanctify the people through his own blood. Therefore, let us go forth to him outside the camp, bear the abuse He endured. For here we have no lasting city, but we seek the city which is to come...' Yes, I will go on!" the traveler says exultantly, taking his first steps into the desert.

As dawn breaks he sees nothing but sand and sky and a path which can be distinguished from all the others by the cross which hovers where the trail meets the horizon. As the day wears on it is obvious that the traveler is weary, thirsty, sick with heat. Just when it appears he cannot trudge another step, a stranger appears at his side.

"Over the next hill you will find a spring," she says. "Keep going; you are almost there," she encourages him.

He is soon lying by a spring, drinking water and eating food which the helpful stranger provides.

"This is the Wilderness of Forgiveness," she explains to the traveler. "People often expect God's forgiveness to be like a beautiful park with fountains and rivers and green grass. They cannot understand why it should be a desert. Yet one has to learn that God's forgiveness is everything— everything! And this is possible only in a desert, where a Christian comes to see nothing, appreciate nothing, hope in nothing but the cross of Jesus." She quotes several passages from Galatians to the traveler:

> But far be it from me to glory except in the cross of our Lord Jesus Christ, by which the world has been crucified to me, and I to the world. For neither

circumcision counts for anything, nor uncircumcision, but a new creation. Peace and mercy be upon all who walk by this rule, upon the Israel of God... I have been crucified with Christ; it is no longer I who live, but Christ who lives in me; and the life I now live in the flesh I live by faith in the Son of God, who loved me and gave Himself for me. I do not nullify the grace of God; for if justification were through the law, then Christ died to no purpose.

"Do you think the apostle Paul traveled this Wilderness?" asks the traveler.

"Yes, he did. For years Paul had worked very hard in the City of Religion, to be a religious man. Still he found no peace for his spirit. Then Paul met Jesus; and from the start, Jesus meant one thing to Paul: forgiveness. He was overwhelmed with it. The forgiveness of the cross was the theme of his life from then on. But Paul's first experience of the Kingdom of God as a reality in his life was right in this wilderness."

"So I'm walking where the apostles walked." The traveler's voice is full of awe.

"Remember when Peter lowered the net at the command of Jesus and brought it up loaded with fish? His immediate response was, 'Leave me Lord, I'm a sinner!' Jesus answered, 'Don't be afraid; from now on you will be catching men.' Implied in Jesus' answer was, 'I will take care of your sin.' And when they brought their boats to land, they left everything and followed Jesus—followed Him here into this Wilderness of Forgiveness in pursuit of a cross. After Jesus had died for Peter's sins and risen for his justification and was about to fill Peter with the Holy Spirit, He said to this man who had denied Him three times, 'Simon, son of Jonas, Do you love me?... Feed My sheep.'

And with this thrice-repeated question and command, Peter's life was healed with the forgiveness of his Lord."

"For years," the traveler tells her, "I've been trying to get beyond theoretical, doctrinal forgiveness, most probably what is taught in Christian City, in order to know forgiveness itself. I've wanted to be immersed, baptized, LOST, in it. I have longed to hear Jesus say to me personally, 'Take heart, brother; your sins are forgiven.' I've wanted to have the blood of the cross flow into my heart and purify it."

"You have come to the right place. Before you reach the other side of this Wilderness, you will experience the relief of having that load of guilt, which still, in fact, weighs you down like a rock, rolled away. You will begin to walk before God without shame. Just as you were once obsessed with the need to build yourself up, you will soon be obsessed with the forgiveness of God."

"Obsessed with the forgiveness of God?"

"You will become so obsessed with God's mercy that you will be free, for the first time in your life, of other people's opinions."

"Ha! Not me." His response is immediate.

"The woman who washed Jesus' feet with her tears was obsessed with His forgiveness to the point where she was heedless of the jeers and opinions of others. Or the cleansed leper—he joyfully fell at Jesus' feet giving thanks for more than the cleansing of his body; he had received the inner healing of forgiveness. When Zacchaeus climbed a tree to see Jesus, he was watching his own forgiveness walking toward him down the road. So obsessed was he with the forgiveness which visited his life that day that the chains of covetousness broke from his heart. You have come to the place where it will happen to you."

The traveler resumes his journey, his mysterious companion walking silently by his side for an hour or two and then suddenly disappearing.

"What joy I feel!" the traveler exclaims aloud. "This must be what the disciples felt as they returned to Jerusalem after the ascension of Jesus."

In the cross-shaped light, the traveler makes out the figure of another woman rising over the crest of the next dune and walking slowly down the slope toward him. He appears to recognize her. From his expression I gather that this person has wronged him. Her eyes are fixed on the traveler as she comes up to him.

"Will you forgive me?" she asks.

The traveler stops still. The woman draws closer, asking a second time, "Will you forgive me?" They are face to face when she asks for the third time, "Will you forgive me?" The traveler's mysterious companion is again at his side, quietly instructing him, "This Wilderness of Forgiveness is not only a place for receiving forgiveness, but also for giving it. This woman is but the first of a procession of people from your past whom you have never really forgiven. The supernatural forbearance which has flooded your being all day is being challenged by the bitterness buried in your soul for all these years. You have to make a choice. The sterile, shallow, lip-service forgiveness of your past life is powerless even to be polite to this woman. But the forgiveness of God which has been flowing in to the point of becoming an obsession can flow out now if you will allow it to."

The traveler reaches out, takes the woman by the hand, looks into her eyes and replies, "Of course I forgive you!"

She weeps. And just as she forms the words, "Thank you," she is gone.

Then the man who called the traveler a fool in the restaurant back in Christian City comes running and panting toward him. Mopping his face with his handkerchief, the troubled man begins to beg forgiveness.

"Of course, of course," the traveler replies heartily. "It's nothing. Don't think another thing about it."

"Please don't take this matter so lightly. I NEED your forgiveness. Will you REALLY forgive me, from the bottom of your heart?"

"But I already have," returns the traveler.

His companion illuminates the situation for him: "He needs your FORGIVENESS. Not courtesy, but active, genuine forgiveness. He needs your LOVE." "My friend, you are forgiven," the traveler tells him earnestly with respect in his voice.

With visible relief the man sighs, "Thank you!" and disappears into the desert air. His companion reminds him of the verses in Matthew 18 which read:

> Then Peter came up and said to him, "Lord, how often shall my brother sin against me, and I forgive him? As many as seven times?" Jesus said to him, "I do not say to you seven times, but seventy times seven."

The Wilderness of Worship

"Water! Who would have thought that in the middle of this desert there would be a sea!" the traveler is exclaiming to himself when next I see him in my dream. From the brow of a mammoth dune he looks down into an expanse of blue stretching to the horizon. "But no, it isn't water," he remembers. "The old man on the mountain pointed to this as

the beginning of the second wilderness." As he descends
the hill to its edge, the strange sea of sand is not as flat as
it seemed from above. There are waves of blue extending
into the distance like a frozen ocean. "Perhaps there is a
relationship between this and 'the sea of glass' before the
throne of God. Perhaps the waves will flatten out as I
approach the City of God."

Suddenly a person of unearthly beauty is standing a few
feet away from the traveler. "Greetings," the being says.
"It's a long way across this stretch. Many have perished
trying to make it on foot. I offer you a better way."

"A better way?" asks the traveler.

"Yes, I have the power to cross this wilderness in a split
second. And if you will let me, I can take you with me. I
can have you safe on the other side directly."

"What must I do?"

"All I require is a token act. If you will merely kneel to
pay me homage, I will lift you across this wilderness with
the speed of light."

"But that would be to worship you, wouldn't it?"

"Why do you find that strange? People do it every day.
You did it yourself long before you came to this wilderness.
The citizens often worship me in Christian City. Some there
worship money—serve it like slaves. Their eyes light up at
the thought of it. But the love of money is only a symbol
of my reality."

"You aren't reaching me with your talk of money. It's
never been a problem in MY life," the traveler retorts.

"How about romance? What could be more beautiful or
innocent than being in love? But when the state of being in
love becomes a goal and dominates the mind, there is
idolatry involved. And it is 'yours truly' behind that idol,"

he says triumphantly. "But the most personally satisfying worship I receive comes from men and women who are pursuing religious successes."

"Well," the traveler cuts his boasting short, "If I have to worship you in exchange for a quick trip across this wilderness, I'll gladly walk, if it takes forever!"

At this, the bewitching creature vanishes in defeat.

I soon hear the traveler reasoning with himself again: "In Christian City it is possible to go through all the surface motions of faith in God while one's real worship, the thing which obsesses the mind day and night, is idolatry. Now that I have left there I can survive only if I'm lost in the worship of God. God has said in Isaiah 43:

> Behold, I am doing a new thing; now it springs forth, do you not perceive it? I will make a way in the wilderness and rivers in the desert. The wild beasts will honor me, the jackals and the ostriches; for I give water in the wilderness, rivers in the desert, to give drink to my chosen people, the people whom I formed for myself that they might declare my praise.

"Perhaps such worship can be formed only in this desert, with its dryness and pounding heat, searing light and eerie silence."

These reflections are interrupted by a sudden crescendo of indescribable music, singing of unearthly beauty. Voices seem to be everywhere. Yet no one is visible. From the top of a blue wave, the traveler sees seven people standing in a hollow with their hands raised heavenward, uttering the praises to God. But the singing has the fullness of a song of millions! Then the traveler opens his mouth and out of it also rushes a torrent of praise to God. In the midst of this music, his mysterious companion returns. Filled with joy,

the traveler tells her, "Do you notice how the seven worshipers are really surrounded by a multitude of magnificent
beings whose voices blend with theirs? I feel that out here
in the desert I have, in a mystery, already entered the
outskirts of the City of God."

His companion responds with a passage from Hebrews:

> But you have come to Mount Zion and to the city
> of the living God, the heavenly Jerusalem, and to
> innumerable angels in festal gathering, and to the
> assembly of the first-born who are enrolled in
> heaven, and to a judge who is God of all, and to the
> spirits of just men made perfect, and to Jesus, the
> mediator of a new covenant, and to the sprinkled
> blood that speaks more graciously than the blood of
> Abel. Therefore let us be grateful for receiving a
> kingdom that cannot be shaken, and thus let us offer
> to God acceptable worship, with reverence and awe;
> for our God is a consuming fire.

After some time the song ceases. Everything becomes
still. No one is in sight but the seven worshipers, who bid
the traveler God's peace and file over the dune, leaving him
alone with his companion. She leads him to a rushing
stream and provides him another meal.

"So this is the Wilderness of Worship," exclaims the
traveler, still in awe from his experience.

"Yes, here Christians learn to worship God the Father
in spirit and truth. You might call it the outer court of the
City of God; for as you have seen, the inhabitants of that
City are all around you. Back in the Wilderness of Forgiveness you began to experience the power of Jesus' blood
cleansing your inmost heart. Here in the Wilderness of
Worship you receive His Holy Spirit. God baptizes you
with power from on high in order for you to worship Him

with a worship which, in the wildernesses beyond, will take the shape of deeds. Joel 2 tells us:

> And it shall come to pass afterward, that I will pour out my spirit on all flesh; your sons and your daughters shall prophesy, your old men shall dream dreams, and your young men shall see visions. Even upon the menservants and maidservants in those days, I will pour out my spirit.

"I have never experienced such worship as this, But will it last?" asks the traveler. "Will I still be able to worship the living God with such grace in the deserts beyond?"

"Changes are taking place in you which, if you let them, will last forever. Your heart is being opened by the outpoured Spirit. Your mouth is being opened to speak as God gives you utterance: 'Your sons and your daughters shall prophesy.' And your eyes are being opened to see visions and dream dreams. You are receiving eyes which see God."

"But don't these same things happen back in Christian City? I am told that this sort of thing goes on in the Apostolic Church of the Future every Sunday night."

"The difference, brother, is that here you do not merely taste worship or dabble in worship. Here in the desert you are lost in the worship of God so that all your praise and thanksgiving goes to Him. Everything you do is done for Him."

"But isn't there a danger of fanaticism?"

"Fanatics worship principles, ideas, human personalities and even demons, but never God. Consuming worship of God is the doorway, not to fanaticism, but to liberty such as you have never known. When you are lost in the worship of God, you no longer worship such things as money, romance, or success. You have found the one true object of worship, and as you worship Him you are fulfilled."

With these words his companion departs. Once again the traveler is alone on a sea of blue sand, lost in the worship of God.

The Wilderness of Prayer

Now the sea of sand comes to an abrupt end in the foothills of a fiery mountain range. There is no vegetation, only walls of dry, hard, burning rock. Bones cluttering the sand at the base of the rocky barrier are mute testimony to the dangers of this desolate land. The traveler fixes his gaze on the cross shaped star as he walks, and recites to himself:

> "Enter by the narrow gate; for the gate is wide and the way is easy, that leads to destruction, and those who enter by it are many. For the gate is narrow and the way is hard, that leads to life, and those who find it are few."

Hearing voices in the distance, the traveler follows the path at the foot of the mountain toward them. There the path abruptly turns into a gash in the mountain. Entering the opening, he listens as a voice echoes and resounds with such intensity that no words can be distinguished. Moving deep into this rocky pass, the traveler nears a huge wrought iron arch under which a man is addressing an assembly of men and women.

"This is the way, believe me," pleads the man, his words now distinct. "This narrow gate to my left is so rusty it will hardly swing. Who in his right mind would want to follow that steep path, when this well paved, well traveled way is open and ready? Come through this gate and you will be out of the wilderness before the day is over. Good food and a clean bed await you at the other end. There are prayer meetings arranged at the rest stops every hour along the way."

Without hesitation the traveler passes under the wrought iron arch and proceeds down the road. Others join him. The route on which he now walks is smooth and pleasant in contrast to the blue sand he has just plodded through. A sign repeats the information that there are rest stops every hour, consisting of a prayer meeting and a light lunch.

At the first such stop he talks with a pleasant hostess: "I've come a long way. Please tell me where this path is taking us."

She smiles and replies, "You will be beautifully housed and well taken care of. Your journey will be over by nightfall."

The traveler walks on, increasingly perplexed. Just as darkness begins to fall after a scenic journey through the rocks and trees, he finds himself on the brow of a hill looking down on a city.

""Welcome!" exclaims a man standing beneath a wrought iron arch identical to the arch through which he had passed earlier.

"Thank you," replies the traveler. "But where am I?"

"Why, this is Christian City!"

Without another word the traveler turns and runs back the way he came. With Christian City out of sight, he slows to a walk but doesn't stop until he's reached the other arch, the end of the false path. He cries out, "I have only one desire: to find that narrow gate and enter it before I take a single rest. How could I have been so blind? Of course the wide gate would lead to Christian City, the place where one can have his ease—never have to deny himself, take risks, suffer any pain or lose any sleep," he adds bitterly.

Finally the traveler discovers the old rusty gate. So narrow he can barely squeeze through, the gate has been almost obliterated by weeds and vines.

Daybreak finds him on a narrow path winding up through scarlet rocks. There is a hum in the air as of a wind through trees, but neither wind nor trees are found here. The hum grows louder and finally can be distinguished as a chant of many voices. Now the traveler sees the people on the path ahead. He has become part of a procession of people all moving toward the City of God. As they walk they are each talking earnestly to someone unseen. Some of them are crying. Some seem exuberant. Some are mentioning people's names and asking good things for them. Some ask their neighbors ahead or behind for help, but their main concern is with their unseen listener.

The traveler's mysterious companion now returns and addresses him. "Here in the Wilderness of Prayer the contrast with Christian City is extreme, you know. There, they do have prayer meetings and people pray before they go to bed. When life becomes difficult, their prayer becomes intense, until the crisis passes. But in the Wilderness of Prayer, prayer becomes one's way of life—the source of one's whole existence. The time has come for YOU to be lost in a life of prayer. Meditate on these passages in the Gospel of Luke," she adds, handing him a sheet of paper on which is written:

Now when all the people were baptized, and when Jesus also had been baptized and was PRAYING, the heaven was opened, and the Holy Spirit descended upon him in bodily form, as a dove,

And a voice came from heaven, "Thou art my beloved Son; with thee I am well pleased (Luke 3:21-22).

But so much the more the report went abroad concerning him; and great multitudes gathered to hear and to be healed of their infirmities.

But He withdrew to the wilderness and PRAYED" (Luke 5:15-16).

In these days he went out to the mountains to PRAY; and all night he continued in PRAYER TO GOD. And when it was day,

He called his disciples, and chose from them twelve, whom he named apostles..." (Luke 6:12-13).

Now about eight days after these sayings he took with him Peter and John and James, and went up on the mountain to PRAY.

And as he was PRAYING, the appearance of his countenance was altered, and his raiment became dazzling white (Luke 9:28-29).

He was PRAYING in a certain place, and when he ceased, one of his disciples said to him, "Lord, teach us to PRAY, as John taught his disciples" (Luke 11:1).

And he came out, and went, as was his custom, to the Mount of Olives; and the disciples followed him.

And when he came to the place he said to them, "PRAY that you may not enter into temptation."

And he withdrew from them about a stone's throw, and knelt down and PRAYED ... (Luke 22:39-41).

And when they came to the place which is called The Skull, there they crucified him, and the criminals, one on the right and one on the left.

And Jesus said, "FATHER FORGIVE THEM; FOR THEY KNOW NOT WHAT THEY DO" (Luke 23:33-34).

"A prayer life is something we engage in alone, yet it brings us into fellowship with God and man as nothing else will," his companion tells him when he has finished reading. "Prayer is going to God, to the Father's door, and asking for bread so that you can give it to your needy brother. When you knock and keep knocking it always opens. Always. Out of that communion with God comes something you share with others. And as you share what God gives you, you have a communion with them. A person will have this communion even if he's shy or clumsy. For this life of prayer delivers one from the fear of other people's opinions and the fear of one's own blunders."

"But does it take these eerie mountains, these cliffs, this continuous danger to learn to pray?" asks the traveler.

"Well, in the past you cried to God in your occasional emergencies. Here you are learning to see your life as a continuous crisis, driving you to call on God day and night. "Shall not God vindicate his elect who cry to him day and night?' The clearer our vision of what happens in the world—how close to the edge of chaos the nations are—the more we understand that the only way to know life is to come close to God the Father in prayer, to cry to Him day and night. We pray without ceasing because the crisis in earthly life is never over."

"But why does it all have to be so hard? It looks to me as though the climb through these mountains is the toughest part of the journey yet."

"Because prayer is our main work. It takes thought, concentration, an active will and the best of one's strength to pray for the hallowing of God's name, the coming of God's kingdom, to pray for laborers in the harvest, or to pray for specific people and their needs. You have barely begun to scratch the surface of the awesome things that wait to be done in answer to your prayers, if you will keep going."

"That's it, though! To keep going. I'm getting so tired."

"This is because your prayers are becoming engaged in the Real Battle. Prayer is the ground where we overcome evil with good. In these mountains you will learn to pray for your enemies. The life of overcoming evil with good starts with asking that good will come to those who have done evil to us."

The narrow path leads to a lookout where the traveler and his companion share a meal. Afterwards they walk to the edge of the lookout where she points to the path winding down through the mountains which diminish in size until somewhere near the horizon they appear to reach their end.

"You see, there begins the Harvest," the traveler's companion says, pointing to a view beyond them. "Remember these words which Jesus said:

> Do you not say, 'there are yet four months, then comes the harvest'? I tell you, lift up your eyes, and see how the fields are already white for harvest. He who reaps receives wages, and gathers fruit for eternal life, so that sower and reaper may rejoice together. For here the saying holds true, 'One sows and another reaps.' I sent you to reap that for which you did not labor; others have labored, and you have entered into their labor.

The traveler looks into the distance while his companion explains further: "In Christian City, remember, there is a fine, wide street called Missionary Boulevard, lined with spacious well kept buildings and adorned with fountains and lawns and lovely shrubs. Those buildings house every missionary enterprise known in the Christian world. There are headquarters for literature outreach, editorial offices for elaborate missionary magazines, and smaller facilities that provide a prayer-letter service for lesser known laborers. There are studios that produce world literature telethons and video tapes for missionary appeals. There are institutions that offer refresher courses for missionaries on furlough, and a computerized itinerary service for missionaries who need to broaden their financial base. There are recruiting centers, rest facilities for retired missionaries, and even a budding record company. But lately Missionary Boulevard has been thrown into a panic by some disturbing news. Word has been received that large numbers of missionaries have committed the unpardonable breach of missionary etiquette: instead of taking as their mission field the approved territory of the known world, missionaries have plunged into the desert toward the City of God."

"But what kind of mission field is this desert?" the traveler asks. "Whose soul are you going to save in the Wilderness of Forgiveness except your own? And when you get to the Wilderness of Worship, everyone there is already alive with God's glory. In the Wilderness of Prayer there is wonderful communion with other travelers, and I'm learning to intercede. But there aren't any lost souls..."

The Harvest

Reaching the outer extremity of the Wilderness of Prayer, the traveler in my dream is taking in his first clear view of his destination. In the far distance, radiant with a holy splendor, is the City of God. Visibly overcome with emotion, his step quickens. Suddenly he encounters a terrible stench of smoke and decaying bodies. Now there are corpses everywhere. Forms with life left are moaning for help.

A woman doubled up with pain begs the traveler, "Please, please do something for me. I can't tolerate this pain anymore!"

"I'm powerless," he tells her. "What do you think I could do for you?"

"A little water is all I need. Please bring me some water!"

"Where am I going to find water in the desert?"

"How long do you think YOU'LL last," she replies, "unless you find water for yourself? Please find some and bring it to me."

As the traveler scans the desert in bewilderment, his mysterious companion returns and guides him to a spring surrounded by thousands of empty flasks.

"Drink some yourself," she suggests, "and then fill a flask for the woman."

After drinking this water, the traveler is immediately strengthened and brings some to the woman. By the time she has finished drinking, her health is restored. Immediately she takes the flask, runs to the spring and begins helping her neighbors. There are men with deep wounds, children lying on their backs with faint, rapid breathing, and elderly people with dirty bandages around their worn faces. Some victims are screaming with pain and others are weeping silently to themselves. Some are revived with a single flask of water. Others need much more. I see other travelers engaged in this same effort. As victims are healed, they, too, participate in the labor of raising up others. As they carry water from the spring, the traveler shares this passage from the Gospel of John with another man:

> Meanwhile the disciples besought him saying, "Rabbi, eat." But he said to them, "I have food to eat of which you do not know." So the disciples said to one another, "Has anyone brought him food?" Jesus said to them, "My food is to do the will of him who sent me, and to accomplish his work."

"I guess we're learning what this means," added the traveler.

He spends many days in that place involved in the work of revival. One evening as he rests by the spring his companion returns and sits down beside him.

"I don't suppose we'll be able to go on to the City of God until we've finished here?" the traveler asks her.

"That is true," she replies.

"But will they wait for us?"

"Don't worry. Just keep reviving these people until they're all on their feet. Then the gates of the City of God will be open, and the inhabitants will come out and escort you in. Bear this in mind:

> Do you not say, "There are yet four months, then comes the harvest"? I tell you, lift up your eyes, and see how the fields are already white for harvest. He who reaps receives wages, and gathers fruit for eternal life, so that sower and reaper may rejoice together. For here the saying holds true, "One sows and another reaps." I sent you to reap that for which you did not labor; others have labored, and you have entered into their labor.

"But these needs are so staggering that I am beginning to feel overwhelmed. The joy of seeing restoration take place before my eyes is offset to some degree by the vastness of this sea of despair. Is there an end to it?"

"Brother," replies his companion, "just as you had to lose yourself in God's forgiveness, and in worship and prayer, you are now losing yourself in the harvest. It is one thing to dabble in the harvest. It's quite another to be lost in it."

"But will I have the strength to keep on working among people with such great needs?"

"Isn't that what Jesus did?"

> And as he sat at table in the house, behold, many tax collectors and sinners came and sat down with Jesus and his disciples. And when the Pharisees saw this, they said to his disciples, "Why does your teacher eat with tax collectors and sinners?" But

when he heard it, he said, "Those who are well have
no need of a physician, but those who are sick. Go
and learn what this means, 'I desire mercy, and not
sacrifice.' For I came not to call the righteous, but
sinners."

"It must have become discouraging for Him, though."

"Jesus wept over religious Jerusalem for its hardness of
heart. Obviously His greatest encouragement on the human
side came from these repenting sinners. Of these He never
tired. You can confidently abandon yourself to this harvest
without danger of being engulfed by it, provided you keep
your vision of the City, and provided you do your work
here with a whole heart. The Spirit of the Lord will sustain
you if you will be careful to listen to these people as Jesus
listened to the woman at the well, to the lepers, the lame,
the blind, the father of the demon possessed boy. Don't be
in a hurry. Take time to listen and ask the right questions.
Find out where people really hurt, what they really need.
Also, you must tell them about Jesus as you go about with
your flask. The water in the flask and this message of yours
are identical. These dying people are thirsting for Jesus, not
theories about Jesus, but Jesus Himself. The message of
Jesus is a drink of refreshing water which brings them back
to life. Remember the verse, 'Heal the sick, raise the dead,
cleanse lepers, cast out demons. You received without pay,
give without pay.' Don't be satisfied until the mercy of
God has raised them to their feet."

"Until the mercy of God has raised them ALL to their
feet?"

"Yes. Think about this passage in Revelation:

And I saw the holy city, new Jerusalem, coming
down out of heaven from God, prepared as a bride
adorned for her husband; and I heard a loud voice

from the throne saying, "Behold, the dwelling of God is with men. He will dwell with them, and they shall be his people, and God himself will be with them; he will wipe away every tear from their eyes, and death shall be no more, neither shall there be mourning nor crying nor pain any more, for the former things have passed away."

As you first experience the labor of the harvest and discover you are actually able to raise these perishing ones to their feet by giving them living water from the divine spring, Jesus, you have tremendous joy. The wilderness experiences of forgiveness, worship of God and prayer have issued in the power to heal the sick in the name of Jesus.

"He who believes in me will also do the works that I do; and greater works than these will he do, because I go to the Father." The challenge is to endure.

The Vision

When I next see the traveler in my dream, he has begun to complain, "How long is this going to go on? I would have thought that by now the work would be finished and we could go on. I'm sorry, but I'm tired. I'm going over by that boulder to rest in the shade for a couple of days."

Later another traveler passes the boulder and finds him lying there almost dead. Running to the spring he fills two flasks, returns and pours the precious water down his throat.

"Drink, brother, drink!"

"Thank you! Oh, thank you! I was almost done for," says the traveler between gulps. "But how did I come to this? What went wrong?"

His mysterious companion joins him again. "Brother," she says, "you lost your strength because you lost your vision. The City of God over there is still your destination. It is your home, the dwelling place of our God. While you work, be sure to take time daily, hourly, to pause and look at the City of God. If you fail to look up in the midst of your labors and see the City of God, fail to stop and hear its music, neglect to breathe the atmosphere it sends forth to you, or to drink from that stream which flows out from beneath its gates, you will be exhausted. You must remember that sustaining power comes from the City."

The traveler resumes his work in the Harvest with fresh vigor. But at nightfall he is overcome by weariness. He goes to the spring; approaching it is a woman who looks to be quite elderly, yet doesn't appear the least bit tired.

"What is your secret?" asks the traveler. "You look so youthful and vigorous while I have no strength left."

"I have taken my cue from Daniel," she tells him. "Daniel must have been a busy man, yet in the midst of the daily pressures he continued to return to his upper chamber where the windows opened westward. There, looking toward Jerusalem hundreds of miles away, he prayed and gave thanks to God. Even though it meant the lions' den, Daniel refused to neglect his prayers. Daniel kept his vision alive by making the City of God his focus. And that's what I do. The more problems I have to contend with here in the Harvest, the more time seems to press in on me, the more firmly I fix my eye on the City of God. I make sure to keep looking up. Every time I eat bread and drink wine I do so in anticipation as well as in remembrance. This is the food of the City, you know. It keeps my eyes AND my heart there."

When the traveler left the old woman, he seemed to be consciously attempting to keep his vision before him. In a low voice he was singing the words of Revelation:

And I saw the holy city, new Jerusalem, coming down out of heaven from God, prepared as a bride adorned for her husband; and I heard a loud voice from the throne saying, "Behold, the dwelling of God is with men. He will dwell with them, and they shall be his people, and God himself will be with them; he will wipe away every tear from their eyes, and death shall be no more, neither shall there be mourning nor crying nor pain any more, for the former things have passed away!"

When I last see the traveler, his mysterious companion had returned with a final admonition for him: "KEEP looking to that City and remember who waits for you there. He has prepared a place for you and will soon be coming for you. Meanwhile, as you look to the City, He will renew your strength so that you will mount up on wings as the eagles, you will run and not be weary, you will walk and not faint."

Two Revivals

At this point I was swept away from the scene of the traveler's journey to the top of a high cliff. I found there a stone tablet inscribed with these words from Revelation 19:

Then I saw heaven opened, and behold a white horse! He who sat upon it is called Faithful and True, and in righteousness he judges and makes war. His eyes are like a flame of fire, and on his head are many diadems; and he has a name inscribed which no one knows but himself. He is clad in a robe dipped in blood, and the name by which he is called is The Word of God. And the armies of heaven, arrayed in fine linen, white and pure, followed him on white horses. From his mouth issues a sharp sword with which to smite the nations, and he will rule them with a rod of iron; he will tread the wine press of the fury of the wrath of God the Almighty. On his robe and on his thigh he has a name inscribed, King of kings and Lord of lords.

Looking up from the tablet, I saw beneath me two revivals simultaneously in progress. Christian City was experiencing a revival which manifested itself in massive and rapid growth. Within a very short amount of time the population had increased tenfold. Building was going on everywhere. New homes sprawled up and down the surrounding hills. But the most dramatic aspect of this growth in Christian City was the appearance of magnificent new church structures towering over the countryside. One cathedral was being completed which had a spire seventy stories high, housing the world's most powerful transmitter. Another church was taking shape in the form of a giant glass dome with a revolving stage and wrap around sound systems. The most unusual one looked like an upright cross with fifteen elevators taking people up to the sanctuary housed in the south arm and a Christian restaurant housed in the north arm. There were Christian educational facilities for every age group from prekindergarten to graduate school; this group sponsored scenic retreat centers in the style of Swiss chalets with vast seminar halls.

There was a feeling in Christian City that this growth was a sign of the world's last days. Books on the end of the age were up near the top of the Christian best seller lists, second only to the Christian sex manuals. Reporters came from all over the world to do articles on the booming conditions there. The inhabitants of Christian City were claiming that when the End came, they would be caught away to the City of God, before chaos erupted.

At the same time, I saw across the desert far distant from Christian City a very different revival taking place with none of the accouterments of successful religion. Dying men and women were being raised to their feet like the dry bones Ezekiel saw. They were being delivered from their diseases, their sins, and their spiritual prisons, merely by drinking the living water from a holy spring. Those who tasted the life-giving water shared it with others, bringing healing to them. As by a spreading fire or a surging flood, the sick ones were being swept to their feet. Laborers there, who had spent years seeing limited results, found that now it was taking no more than a single drop of water on a parched tongue to raise the dying to life. And each day the process was accelerating.

Finally I saw the last prone body raised to life. What once appeared as a battlefield of defeat had become the camp of a mighty army. Suddenly an earthquake shook the ground beneath my feet. The sky darkened, and a sound of war rolled in from the east.

Then I saw Christian City being invaded and destroyed. The magnificent cathedrals, the world's largest cross, retreat centers and seminar halls were splintered apart and flattened by deafening explosions. Dead bodies of the inhabitants who had thought they would escape this holocaust filled the streets. The armies of destruction now pressed on into the desert toward the scene of the second revival. Soon this seemingly indestructible horde was engulfing the Wilderness of Forgiveness, the Wilderness of Worship, and the Wilderness of Prayer. When the City of God came into its view, a single roar like that of a wounded beast filled the air. The horde drove on toward its goal, appearing about to storm the City of God.

But near the walls of the City, the army of revived ones waited poised and ready. When the enemy came within range, the gates of the City burst open. Out marched the Army of Light led by a King of such splendor that the enemy horde had to shield its eyes. The revived ones merged with the army of light and joined battle with the enemy. Three-and-a-half days later the war was over. The enemy was destroyed, and the triumphant ones entered the City of God for which they had been chosen before the foundation of the world.

Again I was swept away to read another large tablet engraved with further words from Revelation:

> **Then I saw an angel standing in the sun, and with a loud voice he called to all the birds that fly in midheaven, "Come, gather for the great supper of God, to eat the flesh of kings, the flesh of captains, the flesh of mighty men, the flesh of horses and their riders, and the flesh of all men, both free and slave, both small and great." And I saw the beast and the kings of the earth with their armies gathered to make war against him who sits upon the horse and against his army. And the beast was captured, and with it the false prophet who in its presence had worked the signs by which he deceived those who had received the mark of the beast and those who worshiped its image. These two were thrown alive into the lake of fire that burns with sulphur. And the rest were slain by the sword**

of him who sits upon the horse, the sword that issues from his mouth; and all the birds were gorged with their flesh. Then I saw an angel coming down from heaven, holding in his hand the key of the bottomless pit and a great chain. And he seized the dragon, that ancient serpent, who is the Devil and Satan, and bound him for a thousand years, and threw him into the pit, and shut it and sealed it over him, that he should deceive the nations no more, till the thousand years were ended. After that he must be loosed for a little while. Then I saw thrones, and seated on them were those to whom judgment was committed. Also I saw the souls of those who had been beheaded for their testimony to Jesus and for the word of God, and who had not worshiped the beast or its image and had not received its mark on their foreheads or their hands. They came to life, and reigned with Christ a thousand years.

When I had finished reading this, as abruptly as my dream had come to me it ended, leaving me with a deep sense of awe, a new awareness of the undercurrents in my own life, and a renewed desire to seek to know God in spirit and truth.

Never has it been more clear to me that two revivals are in progress on the earth. One is the revival of the Spirit of God, by which dead men and women are freed from their sins by the blood of the Lamb and raised to a life which is the life of the sons of God, a life which bears God's nature, manifests God's mercy. The other revival is the revival of religious flesh, a revival which is so appealing and gathers such multitudes and wields such power in this world because it offers all the comfort of religion, while allowing you to keep your ego and all rights to yourself.

Surely each of us has to decide which revival he is going to embrace. Am I going to invest my life in some enterprise of booming Christian City? Or am I going to lose my life in the pursuit of God's will of mercy? Am I going to concentrate on building something that will cause the citizens of Christian City to sit up and take notice? Or am I going to spend my life bringing the poor and the maimed and the halt and the blind to the Master's table?